LEO MADOW, M.D.

anger

CHARLES SCRIBNER'S SONS
new york

143709

Charles Scribner's Sons
Macmillan Publishing Company
866 Third Avenue, New York, NY 10022
Collier Macmillan Canada, Inc.

Library of Congress Catalog Card Number 75-162773
ISBN 684-13688-0

Macmillan books are available at special discounts for
bulk purchases for sales promotions, premiums,
fund-raising, or educational use.
For details, contact:

Special Sales Director
Macmillan Publishing Company
866 Third Avenue
New York, NY 10022

20   19   18

Printed in the United States of America

anger

to my father—
not in anger but in love

CONTENTS

In these days of increasing violence—riots, rebellions, and national and international hostilities—there is an urgent need to understand the origin of these manifestations and to seek means of dealing with the factors involved. Numerous studies are being undertaken, centers for the study of violence have been established, commissions have been appointed, and the literature is replete with articles on violence. Reports on the social and cultural forces which play a role are often pertinent and meaningful, but the crucial factor is the individual—both in terms of his own inner needs and his reactions to his environment. As President Johnson said in speaking of Senator Robert Kennedy's assassination, "It was not two hundred million people who killed Senator Kennedy. It was one individual." Violence can be defined technically as a symptom manifested by outbursts of aggressive and hostile actions, often on the part of a group. Its cause includes social and cultural factors as they react upon an individual and his needs. This is *social sickness*.

Violence is only one level of manifestation of aggression and hostility. Clinically aggression is seen on the level of the individual in terms of personal pathological symptoms ranging all the way from psychophysiological manifestations such as skin rashes, hypertension, and ulcerative colitis to purely psychical symptoms such as depression and attempted suicide. This is *individual sickness*.

Anger

On the third level of the manifestations of aggression in the individual are the sublimated derivatives which are socially acceptable and are often used in learning, participation in athletic events, wit and humor, and daily tasks. These may be lifelong and include constructive efforts of the individual to adjust to society. They may include the drive for power, strivings for success, and creative undertakings. This is *healthy aggression.*

This book focuses primarily on the individual and his needs rather than the social and cultural forces with which he interacts. The chief emphasis is on the clinical manifestations which result from the lack of recognition of anger. If and when anger is recognized it can be dealt with so that it does not accumulate and produce pathological changes either in the individual or in the group. The results can be life-saving.

Although there are definite differences, no attempt is made in this book to distinguish between "aggression," "hostility," "rage," "resentment," and "anger." They all contribute to the fire that makes our pot boil. To show how to recognize that there is a fire and to suggest ways of controlling and utilizing it are the objectives of this book. It is not meant to be a textbook of psychiatry or to tell you what to do until the psychiatrist comes. The training of a psychiatrist is very complex and takes a long time. Some professional people may say that the book is oversimplified or may not agree with all it says, but if it stimulates the reader to look for hidden anger in himself, it will have accomplished its purpose. Proper recognition, understanding, and channeling of this ever-present emotion can change your entire way of life, making it more comfortable, more productive—and even preventing serious illness.

I

how to recognize anger

PEOPLE ARE BORN AS PURELY PLEASURE-seeking animals. They remain so, with modifications, throughout their lives. People would like to believe that they are intellectual animals—that is, that they are governed by their intelligence—but they are not. They are ruled by their emotions; the most "mature" man is the one who has the best control of his emotions. One of man's most powerful drives is his need for love, as is well known, particularly since the writings of Sigmund Freud. But man is full of another emotion which has not been brought to public attention so clearly until the recent increases in violence and hostility. This "energy" probably has a greater influence on a human being's behavior and mental and physical health than the drive for love. It is the feeling of anger.

The history of anger is the history of mankind. Man has been exposed to the effects of anger, others' as well as his own, since he was first placed on earth. From the beginning, however, it was often expressed in disguised ways, frequently unrecognizable as anger. In the Bible, immediately after man was created, anger was openly expressed. The Lord *cursed* the serpent—and also Eve and Adam for having eaten of the tree of knowledge of good and evil. There is a direct reference to anger in the story of Cain and Abel: "And Cain was very *wroth*, and his countenance fell. . . . And Cain . . . rose up against Abel, his brother, and slew him." The first description of the Lord's anger expressed in indirect terms is in the story of Noah, "God saw . . . the wickedness of man. . . . And *it repented* the Lord that he had made man on the earth, *and it grieved him at his heart.* And the Lord said, I will destroy man. . . ." Anger is clearly indicated but is disguised with the euphemisms "it repented" him and "it grieved him at his heart." The statement "I will destroy man" reveals the Lord's true feelings. The importance of anger in man's living and working in groups as well as in his religious experience can be seen from the earliest records. The anger stemming from man's dealings with his fellowmen and himself is of primary concern in this book.

When a man uses a direct expression of anger, such as saying "Damn you," "I hate you," or "I'm furious with you," or attacking you physically, it does not need to be pointed out to him or to you that he is expressing anger. But anger can manifest itself in disguised ways, unrecognized by the angry man or his target.

Our language is replete with masked expressions for anger, ranging from pleasant-sounding but clearly substitute phrases to complete denial of anger. A man said to me recently, "I was thoroughly disgusted and heartbroken. I was so depressed that all I could think of was turning on the gas. I guess I hate you because you have done nothing to help me." Notice the interweaving of such expressions as "disgusted," "heartbroken," and "depressed," until he finally makes clear that he was trying to say, "I hate you." It took him some time to become aware that his feelings of disgust, heartbreak, and depression and his thoughts of suicide were related to hating me and were aroused in the course of treatment.

Over the years I have collected a list of expressions which imply an underlying anger. They fall roughly into three categories.

The first group can be called *modified expressions of anger.* These are fairly direct indications of anger but modified in form. Some are fairly open, such as "I am annoyed" or "I am irritated." Others, which we do not often think of as expressions of anger, are very revealing, such as "I am fed up," "I've had it," "I am sick and tired of that," and "I'm ready to explode." How often have you heard someone say, "You make me laugh" when he is really expressing anger at what you have said or done. Such phrases are frequently not recognized as anger. A housewife told me, "Housework is the most thankless work I have ever done. I clean up today and have the same work to do tomorrow. I'm fed up." When I asked her if she was angry about it, she replied, "No, I've just had it, that's all."

A man will say, "I was annoyed by my wife but not really angry." He is indicating that he is angry with his wife, and that he must deny his anger; the fact that he denies it may be a signal of his true feelings. When a man tells us he does not feel a certain way about something, it often indicates how he feels. For example, if you ask a woman how she feels about a man and she says, "Well, I don't find him sexually attractive," there is something suspect about her answer because you didn't ask her how she *doesn't* feel about him. Why does she find it necessary to tell you what she doesn't feel? Frequently it is because she does find him sexually attractive, but her feeling is unacceptable to her.

The wife of an alcoholic who came to see me because of recurrent headaches described her husband's drunken episodes by saying, "He disgusted me." When asked whether she felt angry with him she replied, "No—I was just disgusted with him." It wasn't until she recognized her rage that her headaches were relieved.

All these expressions have similar uses. They are intended to tone down or deny anger. When a woman says, "I am bitter about the way my husband is treating me," she may be trying to diminish her anger but may be hurting herself more by saying she is not angry, just bitter. But unless she is aware of anger she has no way of coping with it. Not only is frustration a basic cause of anger (Chap. II), but the expression "I was frustrated" is often used as a modified expression of anger.

A second category can be called *indirect expressions of anger.* This group is even more disguised. A most effective expression is "I am disappointed." Indirect expressions hide anger from the speaker and the listener. When little Jenny comes home from school with a report card containing all Ds, her mother may say to her, "I'm not angry. I'm just disappointed in you." She may feel she is being an understanding mother by saying this and may genuinely believe she is not angry. But the expression can be devastating to Jenny and may be less kind than physically punishing Jenny for poor marks. Saying "I am disappointed," without open expression of anger, makes Jenny feel more guilty, and guilt is more difficult to cope with than anger. When we feel guilty, first, we want relief from the feelings, and second, we get angry at whoever or whatever caused them. Punishment would have relieved Jenny's guilt, and Jenny could get angry at mother for hitting her, which would solve both her problems. When mother says, "I'm disappointed in you," it piles up guilt but offers no relief, and Jenny feels even more guilty because she is furious with mother. She can do nothing about it, however, because mother has merely indicated that she is disappointed and may even appear to be suffering—"hurt." The martyr complex is a variation of this attitude which may be easier on the mother but can be much harder on the child. A common reaction to someone who is too self-sacrificing and long-suffering is, "Please, don't be such a martyr!" spoken in great anger. The anger is a reaction to the anger felt in the martyrdom. We often say that we were humiliated or that our feelings were hurt without recognizing how angry it made us. If someone makes us feel guilty or ashamed, it does not generate love for him. We may turn the anger against ourselves for having done what we are made to feel ashamed about. But we must not overlook the rage at the person who initiated the shame.

A patient was referred to me because he was unable to concentrate on his work, had a poor appetite, was not sleeping well, and was losing weight. He had been in an automobile accident a year before in which he suffered a broken arm and two broken ribs. It was clearly the other driver's fault, and his lawyer assured him there would be a large cash settlement, probably $50,000. When the case was finally settled, he received $500. His symptoms followed several weeks later. When I asked him how he felt about the settlement he had received, he said, "What do you expect in our courts? Sure I felt let down—I was disappointed." When I asked if he was angry, he answered, "No, that's just the way it is, I guess." He was not aware how furious he was at his disappointment. Although he had other contributing problems including strong passive-dependent wishes, repressed anger was a major factor in his disability.

Anger

When the user of indirect expressions of anger is asked if he is angry, he usually says "No." It is the *denial* of these feelings to oneself which can create disturbing symptoms. It is not that one does not feel harassed, humiliated, ashamed. But if the boss is piling the work up and you find yourself using such expressions as "I'm under great pressure" or "I feel harassed," it is important to examine your feelings and see if you are not also angry with him. Even if you cannot afford to express your anger directly, you must not deny it to yourself.

The third category, *variations of depression,* includes such phrases as "feeling blue" or "down in the dumps." These appear further removed from anger than those of the second category and are more difficult to recognize. A man who says he feels hopeless will say that he has no awareness of anger, but the anger is actually showing itself in depressive feelings.

A man who takes his car to be fixed for the same thing four times and says he is resigned to it is denying his fury. He may say it does no good to get angry because there is nothing he can do about it. But he *is* angry, whether it does any good or not, and his anger can hurt him if he doesn't recognize it. Admitting anger to yourself does not mean you must express it directly. On the contrary, that is usually not the most effective way to deal with anger (See Chapter VII).

When the depression is more severe, feelings of hopelessness are described, life is no longer worthwhile, and we may say, "I feel like killing myself," or "I wish I were dead." If you feel hopeless, nothing is going right, the future looks bleak, and you are not enjoying anything, look to see if you are angry about something.

Anger may show itself in disguised actions as well as

words. A young child expresses anger directly by a temper tantrum, striking out, destroying a toy. As he grows older he tends to manifest anger in less overt forms. He becomes surly and negativistic. That is, he changes from an active form to a passive one. He does not strike out but merely refuses to do anything, using active or passive resistance. In group behavior, the active, picketing, hostile striker who attacks strikebreakers and overturns cars is not expressing more disapproval and anger than the passive sit-down striker. Both means are effective: the passive approach may be more acceptable because it is less obviously an expression of anger. Adults use the passive approach in the silent treatment. When James Whitcomb Riley was asked how he handled a critic who had been unkind, he replied, "I threw a great big chunk of silence at him."

If Mary has an argument with her husband, Joe, she refuses to talk to him. Since she is not doing anything, why does he react so strongly? He may feel guilty because he senses that he made her angry, and he may try to make up to her to get her talking again, which will mean she is no longer angry. Or he may get angry in response to the silence. Why? Because he is well aware of the intense anger behind her passive behavior. The other side of the coin is seen when Mary nags Joe and he finally says, "Look, what do you want from me?" This sounds like a capitulation but is really a passive expression of anger. If questioned, he may say, "I'm fed up with her constant picking at me; I feel like going out and getting drunk!" but he will often deny his frustration and anger.

Even in the passive form, there is some effort to disguise anger. When anger is overwhelming, or when it is acceptable to us, we revert to the earlier ways of expressing it. If Joe gets angry enough at Mary, he may hit her. Or if he has a few drinks, removing the repressing forces, he offers to lick anyone in the bar. On the golf course it is not too unacceptable to break a golf club if things go badly enough. When driving it is not uncommon to honk the horn, curse, or even cut in dangerously close to a driver you are angry at—or a driver on whom you are letting out anger accumulated elsewhere.

Some of the manifestations of anger are less direct. To forget an appointment with someone you dislike is a hostile act. Promising to do something and then forgetting to do it may also be due to hostility. There are other reasons for forgetting, but anger can be an important, hidden cause.

As we reach adulthood, open expressions of anger are less and less acceptable. If anger is considered as "energy," it cannot be destroyed (forgotten) but must be converted. If two people quarrel, one may say, "Just forget it, will you please? Just pretend I never said it, and let's drop the whole thing, OK?" But it is not hard to realize that he will not and cannot forget it. He may think he has, because he wants to continue the relationship, but the anger must come out somewhere and influence the relationship.

One outlet of repressed anger is accidents. We describe some people as "accident-prone." Their accidents may involve others or themselves. A man who is angry slams a door on his hand or someone else's. Or he gets into his car, drives off, and runs into someone—or backs into a telephone pole, injuring himself. A man hanging a picture for his wife when he would rather be watching his favorite sport on television will hit his finger with the hammer. His anger then comes out in some choice words, anger which he would not have admitted even to himself five minutes before the accident.

An acquaintance who knew of my interest in the relationship between accidents and anger told me that he had had an accident, breaking his wrist in a fall and suffering a typical Colle's fracture, but declared that the accident was entirely unrelated to anger. "I simply went to answer the telephone, tripped over a chair, and fell on my hand, which I had stretched out to break my fall." I asked him for the details. "It was a lovely day. I was working in the garden. My roses were coming in beautifully, and I was enjoying myself. I felt anything but anger. The telephone rang. My wife and daughter were inside, and I was sure they would answer it. It continued to ring and ring. I said, 'Oh shit!' and went in to answer it." He began to laugh as it dawned on him what he had revealed.

Another disturbing manifestation of hidden anger is bodily reactions to it, which have been described as "organ language." Many expressions used to describe anger refer to the body without our being aware that they may be literally true. We say someone is a pain in the neck because he is annoying, but there are people who actually have a pain in the neck because they are angry and don't recognize it. A man may say, "You give me a pain in the belly." Another man may have a pain in the belly and not realize he is saying the same thing. A mother may say of her child who has misbehaved, "I'm just itching to get my hands on him!" Another mother may just itch. An individual may say, "I just couldn't stomach him!" Another finds himself sick at his stomach without knowing why.

A popular expression of the Second World War referred to this type of "organ language." Pain in the lower back may be caused by sciatica, spinal-cord tumor, or a herniated intervertebral disc, but when a GI said, "Oh, my aching back!" he was referring to something he was angry about. A common complaint in army dispensaries was back pain.

Anger may come out more directly and in more socially acceptable forms in sarcasm and biting humor. One of the oldest, most basic comedy situations is a man throwing a pie in another's face. When you consider this, what is so funny about it? It is a hostile thing to do. A comedian may do all sorts of vicious things to another: poking his eyes out, hitting him with boards, bricks, and bottles, and so on. Some comedians' chief source of humor is making disparaging remarks about themselves and others, yet they are considered excellent entertainers.

Certain sports are more open expressions of hostility—wrestling, boxing, and bullfighting, and the more direct participation in killing, as in hunting; these are discussed later.

Why do we enjoy these violent activities so much? What is their great attraction? They are acceptable ways to see anger acted out, anger with which we can identify because it is present in all of us but which, unlike our own, is overt. We tend to enjoy whatever represents our hidden wishes. However, if the hostility becomes too dangerous, the sport may be criticized. For example, if a fighter is fatally injured in a boxing match, there is an outcry (probably chiefly from those who cannot tolerate their own hostility) demanding abolition of the sport. It has come too close to the real thing.

In *War and Children* (1943), Anna Freud and Dorothy T. Burlington wrote: ". . . Children have to be safeguarded against the primitive horrors in the war, not because horrors and atrocities are so strange to them, but because we want them at this decisive stage of their development to overcome and estrange themselves from the primitive and atrocious wishes of their own infantile nature."

This kind of vicarious pleasure—that is, enjoying something because it satisfies a desire in yourself—is seen in other ways. Men who worship football heroes secretly wish they could be one. Women who enjoy gossiping about Mrs. Jones's love affairs secretly desire similar experiences. To see anger expressed so that no one is really injured by it is delightful to most of us because we secretly desire to express our own.

In sum, anger may be disguised in many ways, some easy to recognize, some not. It may appear in language, actions, body reactions, and entertainment. Some outlets may be healthy, as in humor and vicarious participation in sports. In others, we may get aches and pains, injure ourselves or others, or become withdrawn and depressed.

It is frequently asked whether so much violence should be permitted on television. Violent shows are among the most popular on the airways, ranging from war atrocities to detective and cowboy stories with frequent fights and killings. The growing interest in newscasts may be related to the increasing violence being reported, frequently in gruesome detail. Not only are the tragedies of the results of violence recorded, but reporters sometimes badger the surviving relatives, almost appearing to relish their grief. The more devastated the survivors, the better. Opinions vary among experts. Some say violent programs are good for us; others assert that they should be banned. The same division exists about frankness of sexual expression and pornography. Manifestly violent programs are in a sense the pornography of aggression. They frequently (intentionally or unintentionally) titillate our hostile impulses.

I believe the experts differ so much because one cannot generalize. Response varies with the individual. The stronger his ego, the less likely a man is to be distressed by sexual or aggressive shows. He may find them a healthy outlet for his feelings because he can differentiate between reality and fantasy: he can enjoy fantasy without feeling he must or wants to act it out. If he has a weak ego with poor impulse control, however, such programs may stimulate him to seek action, sexual or hostile. He has difficulty in differentiating between what is real and what is just a story and may seek to become an active participant.

Such variations exist in children too, but in general children have less developed egos and should not be exposed to excessive stimulation. Even among children, some can hear frightening fairy tales of witches and goblins and go right to sleep, while others become disturbed by such stories, have difficulty going to sleep, and often have nightmares.

The degree of exposure to violent or overtly sexual entertainment must be tailored to the individual's response. If he is "overstimulated" and has insufficient ego to cope with the feelings stirred up, the stimulation should be reduced. If he can enjoy himself and leave it at that, he can set his own limit. Pornography of aggression should be dealt with like sexual pornography.

II

why are we so angry?

MAN BEGINS LIFE AS A CREATURE SOLELY concerned with the gratifications of his own wishes. The new-born infant's only aims are satisfying his needs immediately and getting rid of anything that causes discomfort—a pin sticking him, a cold wet diaper, the pangs of hunger, or the cramps of a full bowel. Life for the average infant starts out in complete bliss. All his needs are anticipated and satisfied. Before he has let out two screams of hunger, mother is nursing him; if his bladder or bowel is full, he lets go and is cleaned up; he is cuddled and fondled. Before he knows words to describe feeling cold, he is wrapped up warmly. Nothing is required of him in return. This ideal world is necessary for the survival of the helpless baby.

But as the child grows older and is no longer considered completely helpless, demands begin to be made on him. One of the first of these is weaning. Mother no longer nurses him when he is hungry but expects him to drink from a glass. The glass is hard and cold, not soft and warm like mother. Instead of snuggling against her, he is required to sit in a chair alone and expected to feed himself. If he throws the spoon down, mother is annoyed, so he must begin to restrain himself, because it is more worthwhile to please mother than to risk her displeasure by a temper outburst.

Thus, mother, by insisting that he do things for himself

and restricting the total freedom he had enjoyed, frustrates him. The result is anger that he cannot fully express and that begins to accumulate. The process is normal; mother must frustrate the child, if he is to grow up and become acceptable to society. You might ask, "Do little babies really have so much feeling?" Have you ever seen a baby have a temper tantrum, or hold its breath, or bang its head against the wall? The tremendous resentment against being restrained can be seen in an infant who is physically prevented from moving his limbs when he wants to do so. The reaction of fury usually culminates in crying, the baby's common way of expressing anger.

This is only the beginning in the frustrations taking place in the process known as "growing up." Growing up consists of increasing limitation of direct, immediate satisfaction of needs, which the child must learn to satisfy in what he feels is a less pleasant way or to put off satisfying for a while. He goes from being nursed and completely cared for to eating and drinking from plates and cups, to eating at set times, postponing the gratification of hunger until a set meal time, and eventually reaches the stage when he must earn the money to buy the food before he can have it. All this leads to anger and resentment, usually unrecognized.

Another frustration is toilet training. It was easier and more fun for the baby to eliminate whenever the urge arose. Mother seemed pleased, patted him as she cleaned him up, and hugged him afterward. Then her attitude changes. She starts indicating that when he has to eliminate, he should do it in the toilet. If one is not immediately handy, he must wait until he gets to one. This is annoying and frustrating, not only because he is expected to tolerate the discomfort of a full bowel or bladder, but also because mother is unhappy (another way of saying you know what) if he soils his clothing. In order to please her, he tries to control his sphincters, but he doesn't like it. However, since it does no good to express his resentment openly, it is repressed and more anger accumulates.

Much has been written about toilet training and the importance of doing it properly. This is because toilet training is the first major demand on the child to control himself. At these early stages of development patterns of behavior are imposed which become a fixed part of the child's personality. The way these demands are handled affects the way he learns to deal with the problems of everyday living. If parents are too firm or threatening about toilet training, the child may become overly controlled in everything he does. If they are too lax, he may show insufficient control in all respects later in life. There is a fairly wide latitude, but either extreme is undesirable.

Not only does mother disapprove of uncontrolled elimination, but society also lets the baby know he must grow up. If he soils himself he is ridiculed and made to feel ashamed. The cruelest tormentors of all are other children, because they also have pent-up anger that they cannot let out on adults and so choose a safer substitute. They laugh at another child, because they themselves could have done the same and they are relieved that they did not. People often say that children are cruel because they don't know any better, yet if you observe the children themselves closely, you will find that they know exactly what they are doing.

The arrival of a second baby in the family is another kind of frustrating experience. Mother's various demands were bad enough, but at least the first child had her to himself. Now a stranger usurps a large share of her attention, interest, and love. The older child may begin to act more like a baby himself. He may have been toilet trained and will start soiling again. This behavior has two purposes. The first is to say to mother, "I'm a baby too, so pay more attention to me." The second is to express anger. Sometimes the resentment may cause the child to do physical harm to the new baby. This may come as a complete surprise to the parent, who says, "Johnny seems to love little Jenny, but at times he takes a hard poke at her or pinches her. Once I am sure he dropped her on purpose. Yet at other times he won't stop playing with her." One or the other, or both, of two feelings may cause this behavior.

The first is called ambivalence. We all love and hate people to whom we are very close. One feeling does not negate the other; the two can exist side by side. One may be dominant at one time, but the other feeling continues to exist.

The second reason for Johnny's behavior may be what is called reaction formation, a mechanism whereby we act opposite to what we feel in order to deny the true feeling. The fanatically clean person may be denying his real wish to be dirty and messy. The overly sweet person may be denying hostile feelings. Johnny may be showing excessive love toward little Jenny because he wishes she didn't exist. There are many variations of the problem of the new child in a family. A second or third child will have different problems, depending on the reactions of the parents and other siblings. If a child is unplanned or unwanted, he may be rejected, either overtly or by reaction formation which causes the parents to become overprotective. Pediatricians are well aware that the mother who calls the doctor every time Johnny cuts his finger and gets upset because the doctor doesn't rush right over is often struggling with her feelings of not having wanted Johnny in the first place. When anything even remotely suggests that he may get sick and die, she becomes overanxious in an effort to deny her real desire to be rid of him.

At the age of four or five the child encounters still another major milestone in the continuing process of frustration. This is the onset of specific sexual feelings in relation to parents. The little boy becomes more aware of sharing mother with father, and he doesn't want to have to share her. This again is not practical, and he must accept the fact. He resents it very much, but cannot give open expression to such feelings. Mother notices he wants to be close, sometimes almost embarrassingly so. He likes to crawl into bed with her and snuggle up. Father finds that the boy tends to push him away, but if he does so too aggressively, father gets angry. The little boy is walking a fine line and usually develops a great deal of repressed anger.

The little girl at the same age makes an emotional switch. She continues to love mother but now wants father all to herself. She wants to climb into his lap and cuddle closely, sometimes too much for father's comfort. She wants to dress in mother's clothes and take her place with daddy. For children of both sexes the resolution of this conflict also sets a pattern for the way they will react to many stresses of life. If the boy is too much indulged by mother and becomes unduly attached to her, he may spend his life looking for women to mother him. If father is strict and frightening, he may become afraid of men. Or he may become overly attached to father and to men in general, in order to deny his wish to be rid of father. If a girl forms an excessive attachment to father which he encourages, she may be dominated by a drive to find a man like him. If she is frightened by a domineering mother, she may later deny any interest in men and relate only to women, in order to conceal her real wishes and avoid being threatened by mother.

After this period things are "relatively" quiet in the child's life until he or she reaches puberty. By then the boy's body has developed; he has all the secondary sexual characteristics; his glands are fully active; girls now attract him, and he wants to do something about it. However, society says, "Even though you are physically mature, you must not have sexual intercourse until you are able to marry and support a family." The girl too is now aware of sexual urges and wants to test her new-found physical attractiveness. But she is constantly being warned about the danger of pregnancy if she "allows anything to happen." All this may make good sense to society, but for the youngsters, full of feelings they want to express, it leads to frustration. Although this taboo is less powerful today, a great deal of guilt leading to anger is still generated in many adolescents over these restrictions.

Throughout this growing-up period, another source of anger is the reaction to competition. This thread runs through many stages of development. The child begins life feeling that he is the center of the universe, and he wishes to continue to be so. If a sibling arrives, sibling rivalry creates feelings of competition both for physical possessions and for attention and love. Meanwhile, the little girl also is competing with her mother and the little boy with his father.

The awareness of not having what others have often generates feelings of resentment. This can apply to material possessions, to being the center of interest, and to the wish for power. It can create great stresses when it involves our own bodies, that is, when a young person feels there are shortcomings in his physical appearance. The child who feels he is ugly, the short child, the very tall one, the fat one, or the skinny one develops not only feelings of insecurity and inadequacy but also anger. The source of this anger is largely the feeling of not being accepted, not being equal to the others in the group, and therefore not being able to get one's share of pleasures. The anger is usually hidden, and unrecognized. The fat person, feeling rejected because of his obesity, becomes increasingly angry and eats to console himself, thus becoming fatter and being more rejected, which makes him more angry, and the process continues in a vicious circle.

When a girl enters puberty, she is painfully aware of her body and often feels inadequate if she does not develop full breasts. Girls go through torment watching their breast development and have a tremendous concern with brassieres and their possibilities of correcting the omissions of nature. On the other hand, the girl who feels that her breasts are excessively large may fear that she will be rejected or ridiculed.

The boy in puberty is also very much aware of his body, with a marked preoccupation with the development of a fine physique. Advertisements urging youngsters to build up their bodies so that they will not have sand kicked in their faces by the strong young man on the beach are evidence of the strength of this need. A basic concern in the developing young man is that his genitalia may be smaller than normal, and he becomes extremely self-conscious, resenting the inadequacy he feels but which in reality may not exist at all.

Both boys and girls become aware early in life that they

are smaller than adults. The girl is eager to have all the para-
phernalia that mother has and tries to stuff her dress so that
her chest will be prominent. The boy notices when he is in the
bathroom with father that his own genitalia are smaller. These
are facts of life. We all start out being inferior to adults. One
of the problems of growing up is to overcome this sense of
inferiority. Once we have reached physical maturity the physical inferiority is no longer present, but the psychological feeling of inferiority often lingers.

When a child reaches adolescence, he has another source
of anger, which is a conflict between two basic wishes. He
wants to be independent of all parental authority, but he is
still unsure of himself and so wants to be taken care of. With
two such conflicting wishes struggling within him, the adolescent is in a position where, no matter what the parents do, the
result is anger. If the parents are too supportive and protec-
tive, the dependency wishes are gratified but the wishes for
independence are frustrated. If the parents allow the adolescent to make his own choices, to look after himself and take
responsibility for himself, the dependency wishes are un-
gratified. In either case, anger results.

Once we attain adulthood, competition becomes an even
greater cause of anger. We compete for dates and ultimately
for husbands or wives. If we do not win, we are frustrated. We
compete for jobs and incomes. Failure here also creates resentment. We compete for recognition and honors, and if we
do not gain them we become angry. We compete for power
and if we fail to achieve it, more frustration and anger are
generated. Not only do we compete with our peers, but also
fathers may compete with their sons as well as sons with their
fathers. As a man grows older, he may resent the vigorous

youth of his son, since the son is now better able to compete with him and the father is forced to recognize the approach of old age. The son may feel that his father is more capable than he. He wants to prove that he is as good as his father; if he is frustrated in this, anger is generated. Outside the family, older and younger men compete for similar reasons. The same occurs with mothers and daughters, and older and younger women. The mother who sees her daughter blooming into womanhood feels that she is aging and losing her attractiveness. The daughter feels insecure in relation to her mother.

A problem that every adult must deal with is responsibility. Many find responsibility difficult to accept and resent having it thrust upon them. Responsibilities that create stress range from performing the job properly and earning money to support oneself to caring for a family where the actual survival of children is at stake. Resentment of these responsibilities can generate much hidden rage.

At any age, rejection by society, family, or friends for any one of multiple reasons contributes to the accumulating anger. An example is the rejection of a person with physical or mental disabilities. The youngster with acne is an excruciatingly painful example. He feels marked, different, dirty. Myths about sexual misbehavior leading to acne are common, and the boy thinks the whole world can read his wickedness on his face. The fury generated by this sense of being different and totally undesirable is colossal. Another tragic demonstration of this is the epileptic. Until very recently he was rejected by society because of the frightening appearance and possible meaning of his seizures. A mother once brought her daughter to see me because her teacher, having witnessed an attack, told the mother that she should remove the child from school because the spells would frighten the other children. This type of rejection can influence a child's personality. Epileptologists have described the phenomenon of an "epileptic personality," usually characterized by general irritability and other outbursts of rage. Such a personality was formerly thought to be due to actual brain damage related to the epilepsy, but it has become increasingly clear that the chief source of the anger of the epileptic is probably his feeling that he is considered abnormal and rejected by society.

The acutely ill person is also frequently angry. He resents being sick, not only because he is prevented from doing what he wishes to do, but also because he is subtly rejected by those who show overconcern as a cover for their annoyance at being inconvenienced by the person's illness. The chronically ill may build up anger because they are outside the mainstream and no longer able to get their share of the world's pleasures. They feel they do not matter any more and are of no value either to themselves or society. In addition, they can develop hostility because of the resentment of well people at the burden of the chronically ill. This is not to say that anger is the only reaction to illness. Some people enjoy the extra care and attention their sickness secures, and some people truly enjoy caring for others, but it is important to watch for the anger in both the sick person and the nursing one, since it may manifest itself indirectly if not recognized.

Finally, as people grow old, they become fearful of the future and the unknown and also resent the limitations imposed by the aging process on their mental faculties and physical stamina.

Life consists of a series of frustrations, all of which can

lead to buried feelings of resentment. The child who grows up most successfully, as judged by society and in terms of his own functioning in the group, is one who learns how to satisfy his needs within the rules set up by society and accept these rules without resenting them too much. Society does not say that one cannot have pleasures, but only that pleasure must be obtained in a way that does not hurt anyone (including oneself). Freud has described this in "Formulations of the Two Principles of Mental Functioning" (1958, vol. 12 of Complete Works), the two being the pleasure principle and the reality principle. The pleasure principle says, "I want my pleasure and I want it now; I don't care if it bothers anyone else or even hurts me later (but I know it won't)." The reality principle says, "I may have to postpone my pleasure, but when I get it, no one will be hurt." A simple illustration of this is the way one can deal with hunger. The pleasure principle says, if you are hungry, go into a bakery shop, take a loaf of bread, and eat it. You get immediate satisfaction, and the hunger is appeased. Unfortunately, if the baker is not paid, he calls a policeman and you are put in jail. The reality principle says, if you are hungry, go out and earn some money; then buy the bread and satisfy your hunger. The baker is now happy, and the only price you pay is the delay and effort of earning the cost of the bread; you don't have to go to jail.

Growing up can be described as giving up living by the pleasure principle and learning to live by the reality principle. Giving up the pleasure principle causes frustrations. These lead to anger, which can generate "energy." The word is in quotation marks here because there are as yet no measurable proofs of the existence of psychic energy. It is, however, a concept which is very helpful in describing this process. This energy is actually a necessary and important force for constructive work in our daily lives. It can be the power behind the drives to study, to work, to make ourselves attractive, to be successful so that we can get our satisfactions and still live by the reality principle. In this sense, the frustrations of giving up the pleasure principle are essential for us to prepare ourselves for the world of reality. The essence of raising a child consists in frustrating him sufficiently so that he learns to conform and has a supply of energy that he can use for his own development. If he is not sufficiently frustrated, the energy will not be directed to normal development, and the child will continue to strive for the more direct and immediate forms of gratification. If he is excessively frustrated, he may become so angry that he is immobilized and therefore unable to use his enegy constructively. That is, he may develop the signs and symptoms described in Chapter III or he may show such personality problems that he is unable to make a good adjustment to society. Although there may seem to be only a fine line between not enough frustration and too much, there is actually a fairly broad range, and behind the frustrations is always the essential support of loving parents. As long as love is there, the parents do not need to concern themselves too much over walking the tightrope.

If the child in a "normal" household with the usual advantages must develop all the frustrations described here, imagine what can happen in a "disadvantaged" home. The frustrations caused by insufficient love, hunger, inadequate clothing, physical discomfort, competition, and concern about the role in the social group may be multiplied a thousandfold. The rejection created by being a different color or creed or in any way not accepted as equal generates immeasurable feelings. Is it any wonder then that in these circumstances children grow up to be such angry adults?

There is another theme which has been touched on but needs to be elaborated. We all have a general drive stemming from infancy, which must be overcome if we are to grow up successfully. This is the almost constant wish to be taken care of, and taken care of in the manner to which we would like to become accustomed. This feeling has a natural origin. When the fetus is in the womb, it is completely taken care of; it doesn't even have to breathe for itself. Mother manufactures its food, takes care of all climate controls, elimination, and protection. The baby experiences a rude shock when it is born and must breathe for itself, may get cold or hungry, or have pain. However, at first, mother still takes care of these things, and the baby has the feeling that he is the center of the world, with everything revolving around him. In many households this is almost literally so, so that we start out in life with the feeling that everything here is for us, and we cannot believe there is any other world but ours. A good illustration is the story of two little boys, one of whom said to the other, "I was at a party yesterday." The other said, "You were not." "I was so!" retorted the first. "You couldn't have been to a party yesterday," the other protested. "I wasn't there!"

Another great source of frustration, then, is the feeling that we are the center of the world. One of the very difficult tasks in growing up is that of accepting that we are not the axis around which everyone and everything revolves, that there are other people who are interested in themselves and are not particularly interested in us. Unless we learn this lesson, we will continue to accumulate anger, often without being aware of it.

There are many examples of this. Some people overreact tremendously to a lack of service, whether it is in a restaurant, or a store, or having to wait in line. They are struggling with the problem of being unable to see that others have their own world. A recent newspaper report of the closing of a long-established beauty salon, in describing the customers' reactions, stated: "Some are absolutely furious. They have taken a sort of how-dare-you-do-this-to-me attitude."

A practical distinction needs to be made between being self-centered and being selfish. The individual who continues to feel that he is the center of the world is self-centered, lives by the pleasure principle, and often ends with less pleasure than the truly selfish person who looks after his own interests by recognizing that others have their world too. If one lives properly by the reality principle, which is being truly selfish, one can obtain greater satisfaction and accumulate much less anger in the process.

Fascinating work is being done on aggression and hostility by a number of investigators who are seeking the neuroanatomical, neurophysiological, and neurochemical basis for emotions. For many years Paul MacLean and others, by stimulating various parts of the brain electrically or chemically, have produced angry reactions in animals and even in man, although the latter have been relatively unexplored ("The Limbic System," *Psychosomatic Medicine*, 1955). At our present state of knowledge it is probably reasonable to say that these experiments are indicating the mediating structures for aggression and anger and not the initiating ones. Seymour Kety has said: "There will, no doubt, some day be a biochemistry or a biophysics of memory—but not of memories" (*Science*, 1960). I believe that, equally, there may be a biochemistry or neuroanatomy of anger but not of angers. The current studies help to show which parts of the brain are activated by anger, but not why one man finds a certain woman attractive and amusing, while another man resents and hates her.

III

how anger
shows itself
"normally"

THE FRUSTRATIONS OF GROWING UP, AS HAS been pointed out, lead to the development of "an energy." This force can be used constructively or destructively. If it is used constructively, we call it healthy aggression, ambitious drives, the wish to succeed, goal-oriented behavior, and other terms indicating that the activities are socially acceptable and presumably will lead to greater satisfactions in life. If it is used destructively, it leads to all the manifestations of anger from open violence to self-annihiliation. This chapter describes in greater detail how anger manifests itself "normally," which can range from the constructive forms to expressions which are not considered excessively antisocial or do not seriously injure the individual. These expressions may be obvious or completely disguised.

Usually the more obvious the anger is, the more childish it is considered. Children express anger openly by striking out, biting, yelling, spitting—or cursing, if they know the words. The child may turn anger against himself in a temper tantrum in which he beats himself or thrashes on the floor or holds his breath until he turns blue. The last is an indirect satisfaction, because it upsets the parents and this is what the anger wants to accomplish. One of the commonest means of expressing anger is crying. It is a reasonable generalization to say that the most frequent cause of crying, at any age, is anger.

Interestingly enough, it is considered unmanly to cry—even small boys are told this—but for women to do so is perfectly acceptable. If a man is hurt, he is expected to bear it or perhaps to curse. In reality, holding back tears may be unhealthy for men. Crying is an excellent outlet for anger and many manly men use it without thinking of it as a threat to their manhood, and feel much better for the use of this outlet.

Overt expressions of anger are usually acceptable in children; in adults they are less likely to be condoned. Yet many people who have violent temper tantrums are catered to and not considered sick. Such people are often spoken of as "having a short fuse," "quick to anger," "hot-headed," and similar terms.

There are two major reasons for quick open expressions of anger. The first is that the individual has accumulated so much anger that only a little more is needed to set him off. This is seen in the person who overreacts to a situation by becoming more angry than is warranted. Such a person has had many dissatisfactions in life and is walking around with a high concentration of stored-up anger.

The second reason is that the quick-to-anger person has found that anger works and is conditioned to continue its use. If a youngster finds that by having a temper tantrum he gets what he wants, he is encouraged to have another the next time he is denied something. If the next one is equally successful, he will begin to develop a pattern of behavior. Since most people dislike displays of temper, they may cater to the person who behaves in this fashion rather than risk setting off an outburst. The quick-tempered person need not be a very angry one, but rather one who has found that this mode of behavior is effective and is reinforced by further success. Usually the failures are not sufficient to encourage him to give it up. He is often a person who was overindulged as a child or one who found that the only way that he was able to get what he wanted was to "throw a tantrum." Many of the violent outbursts seen in children in disadvantaged homes may result from the fact that this is the only effective means of breaking through the apathy that so frequently exists. Such children may respond to love and affection if they learn that the violence and hostility are not necessary to get them what they want.

Obviously the person with the terrible temper hurts himself in the long run. His anger generates fear in others, which leads to anger at the person who causes the fear, and eventually the short-tempered person will be the object directly or indirectly of the anger he has provoked. That fear can lead to anger is well illustrated by the reactions of the people against rulers who were oppressive (Louis XVI and Mussolini among many others).

One of the child's constructive outlets for accumulated anger is in play. It has often been said that the child's work is his play, which means that his play is very serious and very real to him. Children frequently play games involving great hostility, ranging from punitive games in which one is penalized either by being sent back or being ostracized or actually physically punished, to the make-believe games such as cowboys and Indians where one may get "shot" and "killed." All these games are acceptable as long as no one is seriously injured. Occasionally, as every parent knows, the marks are overshot and a child gets hurt. Children often build sand castles, obviously enjoying the process, yet after they have finished the constructions, sometimes involving long periods of concentrated effort, they destroy their creations in seconds. The child's reaction to the destruction is ecstatic; he probably enjoys the destructive activity as much as or more than the construction.

As a child grows older he learns to express his anger in fairly direct terms, often by simply saying, "I hate you," or "I wish you were dead!" This too fits in with the pleasure principle. According to the pleasure principle, if I am angry with someone I want him to be destoyed. Many a parent has been shocked to hear his child say, "I wish you were dead." This does not mean he is a monster; he is merely expressing anger according to the pleasure principle which functions by the all-or-nothing rule. He is really telling the parent, "I am angry with you." He may turn the anger to destruction of toys, furniture, or books. He may torment younger children or animals, behavior which is often accepted as normal for children.

When a child starts school, he has the first real opportunity for a constructive outlet for these energies, namely the acquisition of knowledge and skills. This is not only a sublimated form of his normal curiosity, but may also be motivated by his desires to compete, to succeed, and ultimately to acquire the tools most effective in allowing him to live by the reality principle in our society. If the anger is more overt, it may show itself in several ways. It is quite natural to plague the teacher, who represents the parents who frustrated him and thus created the anger in the first place. Yet if one asks such a child "Why do you misbehave?" he is often unable to tell, having already repressed the unacceptable feelings. If these are excessive, he may need psychiatric help.

Another outlet for anger in school children is refusal to

learn. Many studies are in progress to try to understand why one out of every twenty children has trouble learning to read. One of the important factors in Johnny's not learning to read may be that he is not handling his anger properly. Reading is especially susceptible to this emotion. If a child is not learning because of an inner anger, it is usually directed toward his parents. The child's failure to learn frustrates them, and this frustration is what the child's anger is seeking. The ability to read is basic to all schooling; even for arithmetic a child must be able to read. If he unconsciously wants to frustrate his parents, he simply doesn't learn to read. There are other reasons for reading difficulties, but this factor may not have been sufficiently recognized.

As he grows older, the youngster enters a phase which is almost synonymous with anger. We call it adolescence, and it is often referred to as a period of rebellion. So it is, in at least two directions: against the authority which the adolescent feels is still treating him like a child, and against the removal of the protection which he still needs. The adolescent is caught in a bind: he wants independence, but he also wants to be taken care of, and thus can't win. This is obvious in the so-called hippie groups. They dress in outlandish fashions and behave in what appears to be outrageous ways, but closer observation reveals that they tend to dress and behave alike. They need to feel they are part of "the group" because they depend on one another for support.

The parents cannot win either. Most parents go too far in one direction or the other. "Okay," says father, "you want to be independent, go ahead. Just don't bother me any more." The parents abandon the youngster, often in anger. This both frightens and angers the adolescent. He is frightened because he really does not feel capable of looking after himself and is tormented by his dependent needs, but he is also angry at the parents, as a reaction to their anger and because they are pushing him into a position where his dependent needs will not be gratified. He may thus go to live in a commune or a hippie pad where his feelings of inadequacy are relieved by the strength of the group and his anger is expressed because his parents are hurt by this mode of living.

At the other extreme, the parent says, "As long as I am the breadwinner in this house, you'll do as I say." Here the father assumes the full authoritarian role; he knows best and what he says goes. The independent feelings rear up in the adolescent and clashes between the generations occur. In rebellion, the adolescent may also leave home and live in some socially unacceptable way, thus asserting his independence, yet gratifying his dependent needs, and always expressing anger against the oppressors.

It is difficult to make generalizations as to how adolescents should be handled, because every one is an individual and has his own relationship with his parents. However, certain principles can be laid down. The goal desired by both the adolescent and his parents is for the youngster to develop a "realistic" independence. Both should want him to head in the direction of self-reliance. In our civilization no one can be completely independent. We need others to make our shoes, clothing, cars, and to serve us in many capacities. But if we depend too much on other people for too many things, we have not achieved sufficient independence and we get hurt and angry because we are constantly being let down. If I go to buy an automobile and the salesman won't give it to me at the price I want, I get angry. He is not taking care of me in the manner to which I would like to become accustomed. He, on the other hand, is not particularly interested in taking care of me unless it means a profit to him. But the person who gets hurt and angry is the one who expects to be given too much (a part of his early experience of being the center of the world), which can only lead to disappointment. Yet if we seek complete independence, it too is unattainable, and we are rebellious and resentful. The object, then, is to strive for a practical independence. The adolescent is not prepared to plunge into this on his own, because he is not equipped to handle all situations. He, therefore, in spite of his protestations, wants the support of his parents while he is struggling to establish this independence. The ideal course for parents to take is to allow the adolescent to work at establishing his independence while giving him support as he needs it, and setting limits when he is too far out of line.

The adolescent has constructive outlets for anger, in schooling, in college, in creating a career, in going to work, and in establishing himself as an independent individual in our society. According to the reality principle this may mean putting off immediate satisfactions but ultimately can lead to his becoming a successful person in his chosen field, recognized and respected, and with an income that can satisfy his needs.

Finally children become adults. Now they utilize their energies in establishing themselves socially, in work, in their families, and in taking their place in society. Anger is expected to be dealt with more subtly. It is to be controlled, not expressed openly. In fact, adults are not supposed to get angry at all. We now shake hands instead of attacking one another. One of the explanations for shaking hands in greeting is to show that you have no weapon in your hand and are therefore not hostile.

Throughout the ages an approved social outlet for anger has been sports. A review of the history of the development of sports since ancient times shows that most activities attended by crowds for entertainment included hostility and destruction. In Roman times gladiators battled to the death as people cheered. Men fought animals until either man or animal was killed, much to the delight of the audiences. In King Arthur's day knights jousted in tournaments and frequently one killed another, the winner becoming a hero to the crowd. The greatest sport for the knights of the Round Table was to slay a dragon and rescue a damsel in distress. This ability to destroy something made heroes of the knights.

As man became more "civilized," open destruction of human beings was less acceptable, and he turned his destructive instincts to animals. In the bullfights of Spain the bull is a substitute for another human being. Hunting animals still has a powerful appeal, as can be seen in the gun and rifle lobbies which are fighting legislation seeking gun control. In modern times sports are much less destructive to human life, but some of the best-attended entertainments today are basically hostile endeavors in which men frequently injure one another. This impressed me recently when I attended an ice-hockey game. The players' skill on skates and their excellent ability to maneuver the puck were a delight to see, but the crowd really got to its feet and became ecstatic when two players began a fight and blood was drawn.

Football is another sport in which men pit brute strength against one another, causing frequent injuries, much to the excitement of the crowd. The appeal of football to the aggressive and hostile impulses of the spectator can be seen after the game is over, when the crowd pours onto the field and destroys anything it can get its hands on.

Another sport which appeals strongly to these impulses is wrestling. Although, like football and other sports, it involves great skill and ability, the crowds are really stirred when one wrestler appears to be torturing the other. In this sport particularly the pleasure is great because the audience frequently feels that it is make-believe, and nobody is really getting hurt, and they can therefore let their feelings out unbridled. Even in a sport like baseball, the hostilities of a crowd can be stirred, as shouts against the umpire and the opposing team show. Other members of the audience frequently get great pleasure from hearing someone express such open anger. When one thinks about it, why should the crowd get so angry because an umpire has called a strike a ball? After all, it is only a game. The answer must lie in something deeper—namely our repressed hostile impulses which here have a "normal" outlet. Shouts of "Kill the bum" and "Murder the ump" are sheer joy to the spectators; yet they are actually expressions of death and destruction.

Fencing is derived from a death-dealing activity and if adequate protection were not taken could be extremely dangerous. Instead of throwing spears at each other we now hurl the javelin. In place of using the ball and mace to kill each other, we now put the shot. None of this is meant to belittle the skills that many of our fine athletes have, and certainly from the point of view of the audience athletics are an excellent outlet for repressed hostility.

Sports are largely an observer's activity, but many individuals who play in sports actively themselves find this an excellent outlet for aggression. In fact, one of the problems often encountered by the beginner in a sport is controlling his aggression. The golfer has a tendency to "kill" the ball. The bowler tends to throw the ball as hard as possible in an effort to "destroy" the pins. The unskilled baseball player frequently swings too hard at the ball, again in an effort to "kill" it. Once the participant learns to channelize his aggression into acquiring greater skill, his performance improves.

Hobbies also provide opportunities for releasing aggression. Building things includes active sawing and hammering; sculpting involves pounding and chiseling; target shooting is great fun for many. Gardening involves considerable physical effort, and weeding gives deliberate destruction a positive value. These are acceptable and "healthy" outlets for repressed hostility.

Unfortunately, the adult carries within him the residuals of many of the basic drives already described—the wishes to be taken care of, to be the center of the universe, to be all-powerful and perfect—and these wishes lead to more open expressions of anger.

A common outlet for anger is driving a car. A mild, gentle, peaceful man, behind the wheel of a car, can become a menacing, uncontrollable, daredevil maniac. He presses the horn before the light has turned green; he rides the next fellow's bumper; he passes in the most hazardous situations —and curses out any other driver who does the slightest thing to annoy him. Usually he stays within the letter of the law, but he is a terror on the road. What has happened? A person who has been controlling his hostilities now has a powerful instrument at his command and is using it to let out all of his repressed anger. He has various rationalizations for his behavior: he is in a hurry; the other driver was to blame; the roads are inadequate; there are too many cars on the road.

The disturbance adults feel over not being taken care of, being "let down," may be subtle—annoyance at someone's not keeping an appointment or at a broken promise. It may be more openly expressed over poor service in a restaurant or a department store. The wish to be the center of the universe may find expressions ranging from a man's being peeved because a girl goes out with another fellow to the extreme expressed by a woman who said that she read the obituary columns and got furious at the people who had died —how dared they do this without ever having gotten to know her! The wish to be all-powerful and perfect may lead to anger at oneself at a small failure or for getting sick.

All these forms of anger are quite common and are accepted by society. Often they can be openly expressed without too much backlash. However, the people who do not recognize their anger are unable to express it openly. They may use one of the indirect expressions described and then say to themselves, "Forget it." But this no one can do. Since anger is a form of energy and energy cannot be destroyed, it can only be converted into another form. If anger is not utilized constructively, it will come out in some harmful fashion.

The healthy outlets for anger fall into two groups. The first includes those used to handle the hostilities resulting from the frustrations of everyday life—the argument with the spouse, the fight with the boss, the disappointment at not getting the grade in school that you thought you deserved. The second set of outlets are those used to cope with the more chronic, sometimes lifetime frustrations of feelings of inferiority, deprivations of the environment, failures in competition, not feeling manly or lovable.

As I have said earlier, the healthy outlet used by the child for his normal daily frustrations is play. He builds things and destroys them; he punches his toys around. He climbs trees, runs and jumps. He plays games which involve all sorts of aggressive and satisfying make-believe actions. Every child needs these outlets.

The adult's outlets are usually less direct but they can be quite satisfactory if not too much anger has accumulated. One of the best for adults as well as children is physical activity. Active sports are an excellent release, and the more action involved, the better the participant feels. However, the activity must be kept within the limits of one's physical condition, and the frustrations of the games themselves should not be allowed to contribute further anger. Football, tennis, baseball, and golf provide good opportunities to let out aggression acceptably. So do individual athletic competitions, including track events and weight lifting. A physical outlet may also be obtained by punching a bag, a jog through the park, or even a walk around the block. Some indoor sports such as ping-pong and billiards may be reasonable outlets, as can card games, but as the activity becomes less demanding physically, the anger may come out more directly. The outburst of a person whose partner has trumped his ace in a bridge game shows that the contest itself has not satisfactorily handled his accumulated anger.

The spectator outlets for daily frustrations have always been used. Today these include observing sports events, going to plays and movies, and watching television. The popularity and commercial success of sports events are indications of their attractiveness as outlets for pent-up hostility. These are socially acceptable and usually keep the level of aggression down to a healthy amount. Some of the biggest athletic events in our society are boxing matches, which may gross millions of dollars. People are generally satisfied if a match is a "good fight," one in which the fighters really attack each other, the more savagely the better. Otherwise, the fans become angry and call it a "poor" fight. They may then get into their own fights, destroying property and sometimes even attacking the fighters. The role of the prizefight is evident from the fact that a bloody, vicious fight satisfies the audience and people leave quietly, whereas a match of expert boxing with little violence leaves the spectators unsatisfied and seeking other outlets for their anger.

Plays and movies provide an excellent release for both sexual and aggressive feelings, since we can identify with the actors. The hostilities and aggressions in comedies are highly entertaining. Tragedies may be open expressions of aggression or death wishes. In the movies and on television the "cowboys and Indians" type of story is still extremely popular. Its characters are divided into the goodies and baddies, and the goodies employ their aggression to right wrongs and overcome the baddies. The story usually ends in an all-out brawl, with destruction of furnishings and a satisfying physical beating to the baddies.

These outlets for daily frustrations help to keep us functioning at a level acceptable in our relationships with most people. The deeper long-term frustrations also have outlets, which can be even more constructive. They are directed toward accomplishing something for the individual or something for society which is ultimately satisfying to the individual. Using one's energies to make a million dollars or to create a huge corporation is socially acceptable. Much of the energy utilized by men in competition with others is derived from the anger arising from the frustrations encountered in attempting to achieve a goal. If that energy is used to develop more effective ways of accomplishing a purpose, whether it is to make a cheaper car, originate a clever advertising slogan, make a suggestion to the boss which leads to promotion, or dig more ditches faster, the anger is being used constructively and everyone, except the competitor, is happy. If the stress of competition causes the worker to scream accusations of favoritism at the boss, the energy is being used destructively, and no one is happy, except the competitor.

A woman may also utilize this energy to develop a career, to be active in social affairs, and to achieve self-fulfillment. But sometimes the anger comes through so strongly that it defeats the purpose of the undertaking. In women's liberation movements the leaders often seem unduly hostile and aggressive. Few people today can quarrel with the desire of women to be treated as equals, but why are so many of the participants such angry people? One of their own arguments is that other methods have been ineffective and the only way to achieve their goals is by direct and usually hostile confrontation. Some radical groups take the extreme view that they can only achieve their goals by literally destroying the existing social system with bombs. This hostility seems out of proportion to what the situation calls for, and this can be seen in the results. The angry acts stir up anger in the people against whom they are directed, rather than convincing them, and then are defeated by increased repressive measures. But the problem cycles. When the activists are not successful, their frustration leads to greater anger and even more hostile actions. The goals can be reached more effectively if the anger is used constructively.

Anger can sometimes be used to accomplish a feat of strength which is beyond one's powers under ordinary circumstances. A person who is angry enough may be able to move something or lift something which he would not otherwise be able to handle. Most people have had the experience of being unable to open a jar of pickles or a drawer that was stuck and on becoming angry enough at the frustration succeeding in getting it open. Here too the anger must be controlled, because if it is excessive you may break the object. A woman told me a story of how anger actually succeeded in making her function very effectively. She had been called as a witness in a trial and was terrified at the prospect of being interrogated. Before she was called to the witness stand she described her brain as being a "sack of mush" and she was not sure she would be able to remember her own name. Meanwhile the witness ahead of her in the case was saying things which were not true. As the woman listened to the testimony she became angrier and angrier. When she went on the stand her mind was as sharp as a steel trap. She was able to testify very accurately, recalled many details that she was not aware she had known, and made a most effective witness. As she explained afterward, she became so angry at the lies of the previous witness that she forgot all her fears. It is worth noting that an extremely effective means of utilizing anger is in overcoming fear.

Constructively used, anger can give strength both physically and mentally. Such normal outlets for anger are dependent on several factors. First, the individual must not be overwhelmed by his anger, because he is then rendered ineffective. Second, there should not be so much fear of anger that it cannot be released directly, as it will then come out in unhealthy ways. Third, opportunities for some socially acceptable outlet must exist. The person from a disadvantaged environment has greater difficulty in finding reasonable outlets and therefore turns to more direct and often antisocial expressions.

Unfortunately, in many people anger is so repressed and so unrecognized that it can come out only in indirect and often harmful ways. It is extremely important to recognize the early manifestations so that the anger behind them can be dealt with constructively, thus preventing the harm that might otherwise be produced. Anger can interfere in the relationships between people, and this is most clearly seen in the area of sex.

IV

anger
and sex

CURRENTLY, THE MOST POPULAR EXPRESSION OF anger in our language is "Fuck you," which, in spite of the definition of the word, has nothing to do with sex.

When Freud first described the instinctual drives, he mentioned only one, the libidinal or sexual drive. He attributed most of the clinical problems of emotional disturbances that he encountered in his practice to the distortions and frustrations of this drive. Later he became aware of the existence of another drive, which he first described as a death instinct. In a sense, this was a drive toward self-destruction, related to the idea that death is the ultimate peace, the nirvana of Buddhism. Freud then recognized that the drive was basically an aggressive one, either turned outward or toward the self. Later still, he became aware that the two instinctual drives, the sexual and the aggressive, usually worked together. His final concept, that there is a fusion of these instincts, has been expressed in lay language as the idea that if you love someone you also hate him, and if you hate someone you also have some love for him. Charles Brenner says (in *An Elementary Textbook of Psychoanalysis,* 1955), "Thus even the most callous act of intentional cruelty, that seems on the surface to satisfy nothing but some aspect of the aggressive drive, still has some unconscious sexual meaning to its author and provides him with a degree of unconscious sexual gratification. In the same way there is no act of love, however tender, which does not simultaneously provide an unconscious means of discharge to the aggressive drive."

There is undoubtedly a fusion of aggression and sexuality in most sexual acts. The amount of each may vary tremendously depending on many factors in the relationship of the people involved. The rapist appears to be driven largely by aggression. The feelings between Romeo and Juliet appeared to be almost entirely those of tender love. Most sexual relationships probably fall somewhere in between.

In normal heterosexual behavior, aggression plays an important role in a variety of ways. If a child sees his parents having sexual relations, he may think that mother and father are fighting and father is inflicting injury on mother. But the child also senses that something pleasurable and exciting is going on and thus becomes aware of the combination of pain and pleasure in sexual acts. The little boy who torments a little girl and the girl who teases the boy are expressing not only aggression but a sexual component as well. When the two are grown, arguments between them may lead to sexual excitement. As Paul Gebhard and others state in *Sex Offenders* (1965): "The marriage counsellor knows how often a fight between husband and wife changes rather suddenly into an almost simultaneous reconciliation and coitus. The fight and make up sequence is common in courtship and marriage. A standard gambit in feminine flirtation is to irritate the male and provoke him into physical contact. This ranges from the childhood, 'Ha, ha, you can't catch me' to the more subtle machinations of adult females."

In the simple expression of affection called kissing, there may be hostile components. These can range from nipping and biting to forcing the tongue into the partner's mouth as an aggressive sexual expression which the other may resent as hostile. A different manifestation of the association of anger and sex in relation to kissing, reported by John Schimel ("Sexual Behavior and Communication," *Medical Aspects of Human Sexuality,* 1970), is shown in the wife's reactions when her husband arrives home and forgets to kiss her. He writes: "I have heard the following meanings attached to the omitted kiss: 'I must look awful' [anger against herself]. He doesn't love me anymore [anger against herself and him]. 'He must be carrying on with his secretary' [anger against him]. 'He must have been drinking' [anger against him]. 'Maybe he's got her perfume clinging to him again' [anger against him]. 'He hates me' [anger against herself]. 'It must be all over with us' [anger against herself and him]. 'Why can't he be considerate like other men?' [anger against him]."

It is not uncommon for people in sexual foreplay and during sexual intercourse to indulge in potentially painful physical acts, which in and of themselves are aggressive but may be very stimulating sexually and are usually within normal limits. These sometimes get out of hand, and result in body bruises and teeth marks, but during the sexual act itself the stimulation may heighten the pleasure for the one inflicting the pain, the one receiving it, or both. This situation has been observed in animal behavior, where the male mounts the female in the sexual act and bites or pinches her hard enough to inflict actual injury.

Sadism and masochism are even more obvious blendings of cruelty and sex. In sadism the sadistic partner is sexually aroused by inflicting pain on his companion. In masochism the individual being tortured is sexually stimulated by the pains. Freud considered sadomasochistic practices the most significant of sexual deviations, inasmuch as "the history of human civilization shows beyond any doubt that there is an intimate connection between cruelty and the sexual instinct." He says: "The connotation of sadism oscillates between on the one hand cases merely characterized by an active or violent attitude to the sexual object, and on the other hand cases in which satisfaction is entirely conditional on the humiliation and maltreatment of the object. Similarly the term masochism comprises any passive attitude towards sexual life and the sexual object, the extreme instance of which appears to be that in which satisfaction is conditional upon suffering or mental pain at the hands of the sexual object" (*Three Contributions to the Theory of Sex*).

The clear-cut role of anger in sexuality was described by a patient of mine, who stated that when he gets angry with his wife he takes her diaphragm from the drawer, throws it at her, insists that she put it in place, and then proceeds to have sexual intercourse with her. As he described it, this is all done purely in anger. The mixture of anger and sex occurs in its most extreme form in rape.

The manifestations of anger in relation to sex differ in men and women because the psychological needs of the two sexes are different. One of the male's basic psychological drives is his need to prove his manliness to himself, which he usually tries to do by taking the dominant role. Thus, in courtship, the man usually is the aggressor who makes the sexual advances, while the woman tends to be more passive, often pretending to resist his overtures. In young people today these roles are not nearly as distinct as they used to be, but the pattern still persists. Some men are interested only in the chase and may not even consummate the act once the woman has agreed to submit—a very hostile thing to do to the woman, who is belittled, humiliated, and physically unsatisfied.

In the sexual act itself, the man must be the aggressor—that is, he must have an erection or there can be no intercourse—while the woman need only be passive. Some men can perform sexually only when they are angry at the woman or when they feel she is inferior or unworthy in some way. This may be a carryover from the time of the small boy's feeling that all women were sacrosanct, like his mother, and one did not defile them by having sexual relations with them. If, however, one could get angry with them or see them as inferior, sex becomes possible and even pleasurable. Some men are, therefore, most successful sexually with prostitutes, often seeking variations of normal sexual behavior which are thought of as belittling or demeaning to the woman. The man who used sex to express his anger toward his wife was primarily interested not in sex but in expressing his rage, showing himself to be the master, and proving his manliness to himself.

The reverse situation is that of the man whose anger prevents him from performing sexually. This not only punishes the man but in frustrating the woman expresses his hostility toward her. The typical example is the man who loses his erection as he is about to enter the woman, or has a premature ejaculation so that the act is all over before the woman has had any pleasure at all. Fear may play a part in this, but there is undoubtedly unconscious anger toward the woman because the result is to deprive her of sexual gratification. In turn, her frustration and anger may increase the man's anger at himself for his failure, causing him to be even less effective the next time.

In the act of rape the male attacks the female sexually with great violence and may proceed to torture or even kill her. Sometimes the rapist combines sex and aggression by attacking the female's sexual organs with knives or other destructive instruments. The psychology of rape is a complicated subject, but it certainly is an overt demonstration of aggressive, angry, hateful feelings mixed with sexual ones. In a sick mind it can be the epitome of proving manliness. Some rapists may be able to perform sexually only when they are inflicting violence on the female or forcefully attacking her. An example occurred with a patient who was brought to the hospital because he had become psychotic. His history revealed that he was a rapist. In one instance he had forced an entrance into the apartment of a young woman, thrown her on the bed, and attempted to rape her. However, he became aware that she was helping him to remove his trousers and actually encouraging him to have sex with her. When he sensed her willingness, he lost his erection. The young woman tried to stimulate him physically, and when this was not successful, suggested that they take a break, offered him a drink, and asked him to try again. The rapist was unable to cope with this, could not get an erection, and left. This event precipitated his breakdown (he was, of course, sick before). If there were a way to design the study, it would make an interesting research project to see how rapists would respond to women who became sexually aggressive themselves. For some of these men I suspect it would be robbing them of the "manliness" of the act and thus be defeating. This method is certainly not recommended as a way of dealing with rapists, however, since it is potentially dangerous.

In rape, although there is undoubtedly a wish for sexual gratification, the most obvious drive is the wish to express rage. The sexual act may be another means of doing so, and the sexual gratification comes from the expression of hostility by whatever means. Physical injury is an obvious means of expressing anger, but forcing sexual intercourse on a woman is also a way, since it is humiliating and degrading.

The hostile features of sexual behavior in the female are somewhat different. The first problem may be caused by anger at being feminine. Some women have great difficulty in accepting the fact that they are women. This resentment may show itself whenever they are forced to face the fact, as at the time of the menses, and they may develop functional dysmenorrhea, or painful cramps at the time of the period. Dysmenorrhea can be caused by organic disorders such as fibroid tumors or engorgement of the ovaries or uterus, but it is believed by some authorities to be most commonly due to anger at the reminder that they are women. As E. Weiss and O. S. English put it in *Psychosomatic Medicine* (1960), "Many patients suffering from dysmenorrhea had been either unusually aggressive and boisterous tomboys, resenting their feminine role, or ailing, complaining children unwilling or unable to give up their childish dependence on their parents and possessing strong needs or cravings for sympathy and protection. As adults the dysmenorrhea patients were deeply resentful of their feminine role or obviously immature psychically and either shy or shut-in or chronically anxious and complaining."

Since the beginning of time, women have used sex to satisfy their own needs. They may use it to satisfy their basic psychological need to prove to themselves that they are lovable. Until this problem is resolved, their interest is rarely primarily in sex but rather in the close relationship with the man which they hope means that he finds them desirable. When a promiscuous woman goes to bed with a new partner, her first question is very likely to be "Do you love me?" The nymphomaniac usually does not enjoy sex but is constantly seeking reassurance about her lovability.

Young women sometimes act out their anger against strict parents by becoming sexually promiscuous as a rebellion and not primarily for the sexual gratification at all. Phyllis was such a girl. She had been closely attached to her father and resented her mother. When she was fourteen, her father died and Phyllis blamed her mother for his death. Shortly thereafter she began having sexual relations with boys, and her mother found out when she became pregnant. An abortion was performed and she was then referred to me. At first she insisted that she loved the boys and had sex purely for the pleasure of it. It took her a while to recognize that she didn't really enjoy it that much but knew that her mother would be devastated if she found out and so managed that mother did find out.

Teasing is used by some women to obtain a favor or some material object from the man. The implied promise of some kind of sexual activity, never given or intended to be given, is frustrating to the man and is a hostile act on the part of the woman. Sexual teasing may be conscious and deliberate, but the woman is probably more often unaware of why she is doing it. Sexual teasing is used by some women to put men down; that is, the woman is now in control of the situation, a position she may be seeking in order to overcome her resentment toward the man who is usually thought of as being the dominating and aggressive person in sex. Men are often aware of the hostility behind sexual teasing and react with great anger toward it. The label of "tease" is a derogatory one. Men will accuse a woman of being a tease in order to make her feel guilty and thus become available sexually to deny the hostility and overcome the guilt. Teasing may leave the man aroused and frustrated, and he may develop physical pains. Sometimes the man becomes so angry that he forces the sexual act on the woman—which may be just what she really wants. She can tell herself that the sex, which is immoral or wrong, was forced on her. Or she can claim rape and show her anger by having the man punished severely. On the other hand, many stories have been written about women who, after being raped, searched their own possible motives, feeling concern and guilt over how seductive or inviting they may have been.

More aggressively, a woman may use sex to obtain favors from men, which may range from trinkets to diamonds to political secrets. Despite the changing attitudes in our society today, many women do not regard sexual intercourse as essentially pleasurable for themselves, but rather as a favor granted to the man. A woman may demand sex as a right but seldom sees it as a favor the man bestows on her, whereas men still commonly feel that a woman is giving something valuable when she agrees to have intercourse. Some wives utilize sex in their marriages, consciously or unconsciously, to make life run smoothly or to accomplish their own ends. Common expressions of anger toward the husband are to refuse to have sex with him, or to tell him, "Go ahead," and then lie back and be completely passive.

Prostitutes dispense sex for money. Many of them resent and hate men, and a number are actually homosexual. They exploit men for the financial return and are chiefly concerned with getting the act over as quickly as possible so that they can go on to the next customer. Frequently, their resentment comes through in belittling and disparaging attitudes toward the man. A tragic instance of this occurred with a patient of mine. He had been in treatment for some time because his belief that his penis was very small made him unable to have sexual relations with a woman. He finally gained more acceptance of himself and decided to try sex with a prostitute. When he undressed, she took one look at him and said sarcastically, "You must have been behind the door when they passed those things out." He was devastated.

The male prostitute often expresses hostility even more openly. He is frequently used by male homosexuals for masochistic purposes, the homosexual deriving sexual pleasure from being beaten by the prostitute. Or the male prostitute may turn on his client and attack him savagely. Studies indicate that many male prostitutes are mentally unstable and may be dangerous.

A combination of the prostitute and the teasing woman is the strip-tease artist who excites men for money but does not "deliver the goods." A physician I know was the doctor for a burlesque theater and came to know the girls well. It was a standard practice to go out with men after the show and tease them into giving money but find some reason for not having sexual relations. They had condescending attitudes toward men, usually considering them "suckers."

For both men and women, extramarital affairs may be manifestations of anger, but often for different reasons. A woman may indulge in an affair not so much for the sexual gratification as because she is seeking a reassurance about her lovability which she does not think she is getting from her husband. The affair may also be a way of expressing anger toward the husband—the woman may say, "I'll show him," and openly flaunt the act. More commonly, a woman may think she is hiding the affair, but her unconscious maneuvers cause the husband to find out about it.

A man is more likely to indulge in extramarital affairs because he needs to prove his manliness, or because he is angry at his wife for not satisfying him sexually. Several patients have told me that they were not effective sexually with their wives but satisfactory partners in extramarital relations. Frequently anger toward the wife interfered with the man's performance, but the "girl friend" was much more stimulating, because she satisfied at least two needs. She provided a means of "showing " the wife, and in addition enabled the man, temporarily at least, to prove his manliness. Usually the girl friends were young and attractive and made the man feel more virile. A myth, undoubtedly perpetuated by the male, is that a sexual outlet is necessary if he goes away on a long trip or into the armed forces, and that if one is not obtained he may become physically ill. This of course is a rationalization. A man also may let his wife find about an affair as an unconscious expression of anger.

The story of sexual frustration is again the story of anger. The manifestation of literal sexual frustration, particularly the failure to achieve orgasm, can produce painful physiological results in both partners. William Masters and Virginia Johnson in *Human Sexual Response* (1966) have described the engorgement of the male testicles and the female pelvic organs; these remain swollen if orgasm is not attained and may produce great pain. But the psychological reaction is much more significant. The reactions to sexual frustrations can range from withdrawal to depression which, as I have indicated, is a turning of the anger inward. Or, the anger may turn outward, in which case the frustrating partner may be physically attacked, sometimes even fatally.

The woman who leads a man on and then refuses sex, or who belittles his genitalia or his sexual performance, may be unconsciously expressing tremendous hostility, which can cause equally great anger in the man. Men tend to regard the size of their genitalia and their proficiency at sex as true measures of their worth, and any behavior on the part of the woman that undermines their confidence can be disturbing indeed. The psychological needs of women do not generally make them as vulnerable to belittlement of sexual skills. A woman may be greatly concerned about her sexual desirability and her physical appearance—in our culture especially about the size of her breasts. If a man indicates that she is not a satisfactory sexual partner, she may be upset but this is because her basic psychological need is to be loved and she feels that if she is a poor partner the man will not love her. This is not meant to imply that women do not enjoy sexual relations or that they need enjoy the physical pleasures of sex any less than men. I am speaking here of the psychological drives associated with the sexual act, which are probably more important in the total enjoyment of the experience than the physical sensation itself. The means used to reach a climax do not significantly alter the physiological intensity of the orgasm. Masters and Johnson's studies have shown that the most exciting orgasm in terms of the effect of the heart rate, respiration, and other physical reactions is that reached by masturbation. Therefore, a man's urge to make as many sexual conquests as possible must have little to do with a purely physical response. If the man has had successful sexual relations with a woman and she tells him he was a fantastic partner, he is on top of the world, because this means that he is a sexual superman. If a woman is told that she is a good partner in bed, her pleasure is much more likely to be related to the conviction that she is lovable and desirable.

Perhaps an example from another area is appropriate. To many men it is extremely important to own powerful racing automobiles, and to drive at high speeds under breakneck conditions. A man feels powerful and masculine when he is behind the wheel of a supercharged car; it is comparable to being a sexual giant. A woman is much more interested in having beautiful clothing or in having her figure admired because such admiration shows how attractive and lovable she is. The greatest frustration for a woman is to be made to feel that she is not lovable, whereas the greatest frustration for a man is to be made to feel that he is not a man. Both frustrations can cause tremendous rage.

Variations of normal heterosexual intercourse performed in the standard way may also be a source of unrecognized anger. It is now more and more accepted, especially since the studies by Masters and Johnson, that sexual play between two people who love each other may normally include oral-genital contact, anal stimulation, and other variations acceptable to both. If either partner believes that such variations are wrong, such activities may be resented and described as animal-like, unnatural, or degrading. The anger may stem from a feeling that the partner who wants this kind of physical stimulation must think very little of the other. For example, a woman who is asked to perform fellatio on a man sometimes feels that if he asks her to do something so "disgusting" he does not love or respect her. However, some men do enjoy a sense of belittling the woman in fellatio and may unconsciously be expressing hostility through it. When there is love and mutual interest, all these forms of sexual stimulation may be a normal part of sexual relations.

In homosexuality there is also frequently a great deal of repressed anger, often near the surface. The male homosexual is commonly unhappy and angry because he is not accepted by society and because of the internal problems which made him a homosexual. He frequently lets out his anger on his homosexual partner. The fact that homosexuals can be extremely cruel to each other is well known; newspaper reports of a homosexual's killing his partner are not infrequent. If a homosexual marries a heterosexual partner, other problems of anger may result. The married homosexual may be brutal to the partner, because of resentment stemming from the social stigma imposed by society on homosexuality or fury at the partner for making the homosexual feel inadequate in a heterosexual relationship. In addition, homosexuals may feel rage at being married when they would rather be living a homosexual life, if society permitted. When the partner is at least latently homosexual, the marriage may not be so stormy.

A problem in our society which has an indirect connection with the relation of anger to sex is the increasing sense of loneliness described by both alienated youth and many adults as well. It is important to recognize that loneliness is a growing cause of anger, particularly among troubled young people. It has been described as "the worst feeling in the world—you feel so awful—you're blue—it makes you want to cry," expressions which I mentioned earlier as disguises for anger. Loneliness today may be a dominant influence among many young people, more important even than the sexual frustration which has been emphasized psychologically for the past fifty years. Lonely-hearts clubs are spreading all over the country. But what is loneliness, and how is it related to anger? You can be alone but not lonely, or feel lonely in a crowd. Loneliness is a feeling of being isolated or apart, of not sharing with anyone, of having no one to give to and no one to give to you. Basically, it is the feeling that no one loves you and no one wants you. This overwhelming type of rejection produces anger which is often internalized and results in feelings of worthlessness, a belief that life is of no value, sometimes even in suicide.

The looseness of family ties and the rapidly changing social and moral values are undoubtedly contributing factors to the problem. The feeling that their parents do not understand them may lead young people to believe that their family has rejected them. They feel that they do not belong in the world of their parents and therefore seek their own world. Unfortunately, the world they turn to may be one of many similarly isolated people who are involved with their own angers and problems and cannot relate warmly to others. Some of these people try to overcome their loneliness by literally moving into close quarters, with many people living in one or two rooms, but the physical closeness does not necessarily make them less lonely. Since the greatest physical closeness occurs in the sexual act, many engage in frequent sexual activity, often going from one partner to another. When men and women turn to sex in an effort to combat loneliness, they are primarily interested in making close contact with another human being, not in sex itself. Sometimes a truly intimate relationship develops and the loneliness is resolved, but in most cases no real bond is established and the seeker is left lonelier and unhappier than before.

Loneliness may be an important factor in the increased use of drugs. Drugs temporarily remove the pain of loneliness. Alcohol is sometimes used for the same purpose. If the rage generated by loneliness is turned outward, the individual may become destructive toward everything that has rejected him, either specific persons or society as a whole. If it is turned inward, he becomes depressed and may even do away with himself.

In the proper proportion, a mixture of aggression and sex can lead to a very healthy and satisfying relationship between two people. In fact, if there is not a certain amount of aggression, the sexual act cannot take place and if intercourse is attempted, it may be unsatisfactory. When sex and anger are not in proportion, or sex is used primarily as an outlet for hostility, problems arise. Here again the important factor is to recognize the anger when it exists and to deal with it in a more constructive way. If this is not done, the aggression can lead to great unhappiness and also destroy the enjoyment of sex itself.

V

how anger can hurt us

MAN IS AN EXTREMELY COMPLEX EMOTIONAL organism, and the way in which he copes with his emotions is probably what separates him most widely from the rest of the animal kingdom. His greatest pleasures in life come from the realistic fulfillment of his emotional drives. If his emotions are mishandled, however, this not only can lead to unhappiness but also may actually interfere with the normal healthy functioning of his body. One of the emotions that can cause the greatest harm is anger. There are plenty of organic causes for illnesses, and no one should attempt to diagnose or treat himself. If you become ill, you should consult your physician and follow his instructions. However, unrecognized anger can contribute to many physical disabilities, and its recognition may help to alleviate a significant portion of the problem.

Anger can affect us adversely both physically and mentally. If we think of it as a form of energy which if repressed must come out somewhere, we must recognize that it can harm almost any part of our body or influence our emotions and eventually our minds if a sufficient amount is accumulated. Flanders Dunbar wrote in *Psychiatry in the Medical Specialties* (1959): "The task of the physician is to enable man through understanding of the laws governing his energy economy to use energy for healthy living. Energy misused creates susceptibility to diseases and endangers life."

Anger

There are two nervous systems which regulate the functioning of the human body. One, called the parasympathetic system, maintains such everyday activities as digestion of food and any recuperative processes that are needed. The other, the sympathetic nervous system, is the emergency system, which mobilizes those forces necessary to meet a sudden demand. The two may be compared to the functions in a country in peacetime versus those in wartime. During peace, the nation grows by building roads, towns, and public utilities. It maintains its daily functions of providing food, education, policing, and care for the sick. It develops such projects as recreational activities and space exploration. If the country goes to war, an emergency is declared, and most of the nation's energies are mobilized to fight the war. Instead of being spent on building cities and parks, money is used for weapons. Young men cannot complete their education because they are needed as soldiers. People may even have to go hungry because the funds have been diverted to guns and bullets. Similarly, when man's emergency nervous system is stimulated, preparations are made in his body to make most available whatever may be needed to deal with the emergency. He can handle the sudden demand in one of two ways, either of which requires a great deal of energy. He may stand up to the stress and fight it in some way or he may withdraw —the so-called fight-or-flight reaction. Either way he needs all the changes brought about by the sympathetic nervous system to be able to cope with the situation.

This sympathetic system is, however, a primitive mechanism designed to deal with the kind of physical emergencies that confronted our ancestors when lions came charging at them. If men did not react quickly enough, they did not survive. Today, despite the fact that there are relatively few wild animals attacking us, literally at least, the sympathetic nervous system still reacts in our bodies in the full mobilizing way of eons ago.

Thus, if we get angry, our body prepares for action, and a number of changes take place inside us. More sugar pours into our system so we have more energy. More blood, containing needed nourishment, is circulated by increasing the blood pressure and making the heart beat faster. More adrenalin is secreted, to dilate the pupils of the eyes and make us see better, and to help mobilize other such needed activities. If there is no discharge of this build-up, as is usually the case, we remain in a chronic state of preparedness, with heart beating rapidly, blood pressure up, and chemical changes in the blood, and eventually this condition can harm us physically.

headache

Although there are many known organic causes of headache, including meningitis, brain tumors, abscesses, hemorrhages, by far the most common cause is tension. Allergies and eyestrain are frequently considered to be causes of headache, but emotions are probably more often responsible. Tension is probably most often created by repressed anger. Our language reveals this when we speak of expressing anger by "blowing my top," "I felt the top of my head would come off," a "blinding rage," and so on.

Pain of emotional origin is most frequently the result of anger that has been turned against the self. Hurting someone is usually a manifestation of anger toward that individual; hurting oneself therefore shows anger toward the self.

The hurting may be direct—striking oneself in the face or head or accidentally catching a finger in a door—or indirect —turning anger inside and developing a severe headache. One patient told me that, in a situation which stirred up tremendous anger, she was usually able to handle the problem calmly. The next day, however, she was certain to have a "splitting headache." While she was occupied, she had no symptoms, but once she was out of the active situation the headache struck. The tension headache is often described as a feeling of a very tight skull cap or a band around the head, squeezing it. The pains frequently go down the back of the neck and are sometimes attributed to muscle disease or a pinched nerve, but probably the commonest cause is muscle tension resulting from accumulated hidden anger. When we say that someone "gives us a pain in the neck," we don't mean he is pinching our cervical nerves—we mean he is making us angry.

gastrointestinal disorders

One system of the body frequently used as an outlet for repressed anger is the gastrointestinal tract, which extends from the mouth to the rectum. This tract is phylogenetically the oldest system in the body and is therefore most commonly used as an outlet for our emotions when they cannot be expressed in other ways. This includes not only expressions of love and affection—"my bowels yearned for her"—but anger as well. When the gastrointestinal system reacts to deal with one of these emotions, it is unable to handle the need but continues to maintain the changes it has undergone. Pain then occurs and illness may develop. This thirty-foot-long tube is particularly prone to react to repressed rage, and the manifestations take various forms depending on the part of the tract involved. Dentists are well aware that emotional problems may manifest themselves in toothache and other oral complaints. Some people have difficulty swallowing. The cause may be esophageal spasms, but these can result from the inability to "swallow" any more anger.

The stomach also may be involved. Nausea and vomiting may be an expression of not being able to "stomach something." People described as having "weak stomachs" throw up for slight cause; one factor to be considered in these individuals is hidden anger.

A special type of nausea is the "morning sickness" of the pregnant woman. Physiological explanations for this include hormonal factors and the pressure of the growing child on the gastrointestinal tract, and sometimes women have morning sickness before they know they are pregnant. However, a cause of persistent morning sickness may be an unconscious wish to be rid of the child—not being able to "stomach" the pregnancy. A woman who did not want to become pregnant may literally be trying to vomit out the fetus. Since the wish is unconscious, she can deny it quite honestly. The anger can only be revealed indirectly or come out against other people, which is more acceptable than facing anger over being pregnant.

An interesting psychosomatic disturbance is the gastric ulcer. There are many theories about the cause of ulcers, and the treatment may be medical, surgical, or both. However, an essential ingredient in practically all ulcers is the emotional factor, which again is frequently repressed anger. One of the psychological causes of ulcers shows a distinctive pattern. The person who develops an ulcer from emotional causes is one who is basically dependent and wants to be mothered. However, he cannot tolerate these dependency wishes and becomes angry at himself for wanting to be cared for like a baby. This anger is probably one of the essential factors in the development of ulcers. Even the treatment suggests the wish to be mothered; the medical regimen which is still one of the most effective is milk and cream, the diet of a baby. As H. G. Wolff wrote in *Stress and Disease* (1953): "One of the earliest aggressive patterns manifesting itself in the infant is associated with hunger and eating. This pattern may reassert itself in certain individuals in later life when they feel threatened. At such times of danger, feelings of anger and deprivation, of longing for emotional support, or of need to be 'cared for' may be repressed by the individual with an equally insistent assertion that he is strong, independent, capable of doing alone or 'standing on his own feet.' Either through actual deprivation of emotional support, an unwillingness to accept it or through other frustrations, this feeling state shows itself in the stomach as one of the readiness for eating. The gastric hyperfunction associated with this reaction pattern is manifested by increased blood flow, motility and acid secretion. Under such circumstances the mucous membrane was found to be unusually fragile. Hemorrhage, erosion and ulceration readily ensued. The hyperdynamic state of the stomach when sustained was found to be associated with symptoms, namely heartburn and localized epigastric pain, relieved by food and soda whether or not ulceration was present."

Another area of the gastrointestinal tract frequently affected by anger is the lower bowel or colon. This is seen very clearly from the number of expressions of anger in our languages that refer to the large colon and its products. Some people use these phrases to express anger; others develop constipation (remain full of feces), of diarrhea (an attempt to defecate on the hated one or a wish to be rid of the disturbance).

Ulcerative colitis may be caused by infections or allergies, but probably the most common cause is repressed anger. Colitis may be a carryover from childhood, when a bowel movement had a mixture of meanings. On the one hand, it could be a gift to the parent; on the other hand, if the child wished to express anger toward his parents, one method of doing so was to soil himself. This imposed on his parents the burden of cleaning him up, drew attention and possible affection, created embarrassment if others were present, and so on, but this action was still a more acceptable expression than open hostility. Striking the parent or breaking something would have brought about a more serious punishment. However, parents are frequently aware that soiling is an expression of anger and punish the child for it, expressing their own anger at the act itself and at having to clean the child up, but also probably an instinctive recognition of the child's anger. As we get older we may not actually soil ourselves, but as anger accumulates it may manifest itself in diarrhea and cramps. The anger now has been turned inward, and the angry one has pain and the discomfort of having to evacuate so frequently that he may debilitate himself seriously. If this type of colitis persists, severely disabling chronic illness and possibly even death may result.

Many people with mild hemorrhoids have found that these get much worse when they are angry, and the severity of the hemorrhoidal symptoms is a measure of how angry they are.

respiratory disorders

Another body system which can be affected by repressed anger is the respiratory system. The most frequent disease of mankind—the common cold—is probably related to the effects of repressed anger. Modern medical science theorizes that most people carry the viruses that cause a cold around in their bodies all the time. Why, then, do we not have colds all the time? The theory proposes that people normally have a high resistance to the viruses. If we are exposed to another person with a cold, we may get a dose of the viruses sufficient to overwhelm normal resistance. Or resistance may be lowered by other factors, and then the viruses attack, producing the symptoms of an upper respiratory infection—running nose, sore throat, and cough. In dealing with colds the fact that viruses cause them is less important than the question of what lowers the resistance. If we get chilled or expose ourselves to marked alterations of temperature or accumulate excessive fatigue, resistance may be lowered and a cold may develop. However, people who have been out skiing, enjoying themselves and obviously under no emotional stress, may be chilled and exhausted and yet not take cold. Although much more research is needed, many people are aware that they develop colds after emotional frustration. Resistance may be lowered because of the emotional stress, and one of the common stressful emotions is anger.

A much more serious respiratory disturbance which may be related to anger is asthma. Here again numerous medical factors are considered in the etiology of asthma, including allergies and infections. But just as breath-holding in children is a form of temper tantrum, so when anger is repressed or accumulates and is then set off by an acute episode, the individual may develop a severe asthmatic attack.

I have seen patients develop nasal congestion and mucoid discharge when talking about an unhappy marriage or anger at parents or at someone who has hurt them. One woman had an asthmatic attack in the middle of such an interview.

skin disorders

Repressed anger can also affect the skin. One of the most common dermatological conditions is pruritus or itching. If a person has chronic itch, scratching may cause a break in the skin which leads to a secondary infection, and what is known as neurodermatitis or dermatitis factitia, which means a dermatitis created by the individual, may develop. We speak of "itching to get our hands on someone," as an expression of anger. When the anger is repressed, it may lead to literally attacking our own skin. Sometimes anger against oneself because of feelings of guilt is taken out on one's own dermis. Neurodermatitis may occur anywhere on the body. One form which is especially disabling and uncomfortable is pruritus ani, or itching around the rectal area. This can be very embarrassing because it is almost uncontrollable. Itching of the female genitalia, called pruritus vulva, is equally embarrassing and is probably of a similar etiology.

Hives is another dermatological condition which may be caused by the "germs" of anger. Wolff, in the work previously cited, describes an experiment proving the role of anger in hives. With a patient who had hives he "introduced as a topic for discussion a painful family situation, causing the patient to feel as though he were being struck. 'Just thinking about the things they did to me' was his answer when asked about his attitude at this moment. [Note the implied anger.] Simultaneously, the capillaries of the forearm behaved as though he actually had been struck, their tone fell and weals developed, in this instance called 'hives.' " Wolff also reported recordings of conversation during urticarial reactions which included such remarks as "They did a lot of things to me and I couldn't do anything about it," "I was getting pushed around," "I had to sit and take it," "I was taking a beating," "He knocked me down and walked all over me." The reaction could only have been fury, but this is described in terms of frustration and helplessness against the attacks. We now know that such feelings lead to vast quantities of repressed anger.

genito-urinary disorders

Still another system which may be affected by anger is the genito-urinary tract. A common expression of anger is "piss on him!" and some people must urinate frequently because of repressed anger. A variation is to tell someone to "hold your water" when you want him to withhold anger.

Although fear is commonly involved in a man's inability to have an erection or in causing frigidity on the part of the woman, anger may also be extremely important. I have mentioned that a man may lose his erection because of repressed anger toward the woman. She is left unsatisfied, and the effect is comparable to that of any other expression of anger including physical punishment. A woman may have unconscious anger at being penetrated and therefore go into a spasm which does not permit the man to enter. It has already been noted that anger can cause many sexual problems that manifest themselves in physical symptoms.

arthritis

Although there are many causes for arthritis and many forms of the disease, repressed anger is certainly a contributing factor. Several authorities have reported observing rheumatoid arthritis related to emotional factors, particularly hostility. It may occur in women who unconsciously resent men and who are therefore in a chronic state of repressed anger. If we are angry with a person, we may say, "If I get my hands on him, I'll cripple him!" This is exactly what arthritis does to the individual who turns the anger against himself.

disabilities of the nervous system

Also susceptible to repressed anger is the nervous system itself. The neurologist is well aware of anger's role in headaches and backaches; it may also be important to look for its possible contribution to the precipitation of other neurological conditions, such as strokes, tics of various sorts, and speech disturbances, including stuttering and stammering. The expression "speechless with rage" suggests the possible effect of anger on speech. Some neurological diseases such as epileptic seizures tend to have repeated episodes. Emotions, particularly repressed anger, can set off such a seizure. The individual may also develop an epileptic personality because of his anger. In one study a known epileptic was connected to an electroencephalograph, a machine which measures brain waves and shows characteristic changes for epilepsy. His brain waves were normal. He was then engaged in a conversation that made him angry. His brain waves began to change and he had a seizure. This clearly demonstrates how anger can precipitate a change in the electrical activity of the brain and, in a susceptible individual, can actually bring on a convulsion. Not all seizures are brought on by anger, but it may be a precipitating factor which, when recognized, can be helpful in treatment.

In multiple sclerosis and other conditions which tend to have exacerbations and remissions, repressed anger may contribute to the onset of an attack.

circulatory disorders

Vacillations in blood pressure are a common outlet for anger. Our language reveals this in such comments as "Don't get your blood pressure up," "Don't get hyper" (meaning "Don't get hypertense"), and others. Although several types of hypertension have been shown to be due to specific organic factors, probably a frequent cause is repressed anger.

As mentioned earlier, one of the most important reactions in preparing the body for an emergency is an elevation of blood pressure. If the danger is not resolved or is unrecognized, the stress continues and the high blood pressure persists, eventually resulting in a chronic state of hypertension. The problem is usually a conflict between a wish to be aggressive and a need to repress the aggressive drives, out of fear, guilt, or a wish for approval. The conflict keeps the sympathetic system stimulated and hypertension results.

The general manager of a large corporation told me that his blood pressure was going up and that he had been treated medically for two years. In telling the story he indicated the stresses he had been under, both from employees who constantly harassed him for higher salaries and better working conditions and threatened strikes and walkouts and from customers who were dissatisfied with the service and complained about defective merchandise and the company's lack of interest in satisfying their demands. In addition, the board of the corporation wanted to know why he was not making higher profits. When I asked how he felt about this situation, he said, "Oh, these are the vagaries of modern life and I suppose this is just the direction our society is taking." When I specifically asked him about anger, he said that he understood the pressures of doing business and accepted them. However, his blood pressure had gone from a normal 120 over 80 to 240 over 110.

In an individual with coronary artery disease, anginal attacks may be precipitated by emotions, particularly anger, and the role of anger in coronary thrombosis is fairly well accepted. Several of my medical colleagues, in attempts to dispute the role of anger, have cited examples of calm, placid, relaxed men who had coronary occlusions. If such individuals are studied more closely, however, they are found to be people who never expressed their anger. The outward manifestation of super placidity is a tipoff to the fact that these people are repressing vast quantities of anger. They are too well controlled and eventually build up a powder keg of anger which, in combination with diseased coronary arteries, produces disastrous results.

An important note of caution must be sounded at this point. I have said that anger is a form of energy, which, if repressed, may come out in somatic manifestations. If the somatic symptom clears up but the anger persists, it may come out in still another form which can be equally or even more harmful. Cases have occurred where a patient had a psychosomatic condition such as ulcerative colitis but except for the colitis was quite peaceful. If the anger becomes too great, the somatic symptom may not be able to handle the stress and may disappear. But the patient then becomes depressed and may even attempt suicide. That is, if the individual's anger is being expressed in bodily symptoms, he may outwardly be at peace with himself and the world. However, the combination of tranquility with a psychosomatic type of disorder must make one suspect that some repressed emotion is being handled by the somatic manifestations. Merely removing the symptom may lead to a marked emotional turmoil, because the anger still exists and must come out somehow.

The reverse of this situation is less common but occurred recently in a patient who was admitted to the hospital because of an acute asthmatic attack. She had lost her husband two years earlier and had become depressed. Treatment with electric shock had cleared up the depression, but she then developed asthmatic attacks. The basic anger had not been removed. While electric shock may be a good treatment for depression when properly used, and the only effectual therapy in certain cases, it is more desirable, where possible, to treat and remove the underlying cause.

Hemorrhage of the brain is usually caused by a combination of hypertension and cerebral arteriosclerosis. It is sometimes called apoplexy or stroke and may have a strong emotional component, as is shown by such expressions as "apoplectic with rage" and "Don't get so mad, you'll burst a blood vessel!" Anger can produce the hypertension which explodes the diseased cerebral artery, and a stroke results.

anger as a reaction to physical sickness

Not only does repressed anger produce physical symptoms from headaches to hemorrhoids, but it can also seriously aggravate already existing physical illnesses. Even if the illness is organic, anger can play an important role in how we respond to it. If we get angry at having a physical sickness and being disabled, unable to work, with added financial burdens, the anger can prolong both illness and convalescence. How often are people described as grouchy and impossible when they are ill? They become demanding, childish, irritable, and prone to outbursts of temper. It is essential to be aware of anger at being sick so that it will not work against you. It is not enough to know that you are angry, you must recognize that the anger is at being sick. It is also extremely important that people close to the sick one involved in the demands of nursing care, concerned about expenses and the threat of the loss of a loved one, be aware of the anger this can generate, anger which they must deny because of their guilt about such feelings. Such anger must not be hidden from oneself, though it probably should not be expressed directly to the patient. If you refuse to recognize it in yourself, it is bound to come out indirectly and thus work against the patient's best interest. If a man has unacknowledged anger about his wife's illness, he may forget to get her medicine or find that, because of work to be done at the office he cannot come home and help her, or even not feel well himself. One of the problems with this source of anger, as with many others, is feeling guilt over anger. But an attempt to be reasonable only confuses the issue. The real matter to be decided is what your true feelings are. If you can admit them to yourself, you are in a better position to deal with them.

anger and emotional disturbances

As extensive as are the effects of repressed anger on our physical being, their influence on our emotional lives, and therefore our lives generally, is even more pervading. The ability to enjoy what we are doing, our daily living, and our planning for the future are constantly influenced by this emotion.

In addition to the whole range of somatic manifestations, there is also a broad spectrum of emotional disturbances from withheld rage, extending from brief episodes of impaired judgment with harmful consequences to profound depression and suicide. A child has a toy that doesn't work, so he smashes it. A teenager gets angry because a teacher scolded him and quits school. A young woman has a quarrel with her boy friend, picks up a man at a bar, goes to bed with him, and becomes pregnant. A junior partner has an argument with the senior partner and offers to sell out for much less than the business is worth. Two men get into a fistfight and one strikes his head against the pavement and dies. At all ages, anger influences our thinking and our actions and the undesirable results can range from the loss of a toy to the loss of a life.

When anger is turned inward, it can produce a whole gamut of clinical emotional disturbances, usually variations of depression. As indicated in Chapter I, there are many expressions for mood alterations actually related to depression. Everyone has such feelings at times, and they do not necessarily mean that one is clinically ill. "Blue Monday" is probably related to having to go back to work after a weekend of freedom. We may not be aware that we are angry about having to get back to work or about the tasks to be faced, but this unconscious anger manifests itself in Monday "blues."

If sufficient anger is accumulated or a person encounters experiences that are particularly anger-provoking, he may develop the condition that is called a depression. Depression is a clinical syndrome which manifests itself by a variety of symptoms, including general malaise, insomnia, poor appetite, and feelings of hopelessness. The person describes himself as worthless, blames himself for everything that is wrong, and in extreme cases may commit suicide.

Clinically, depressions can be classified according to degree and cause. They are sometimes divided into neurotic depressions and psychotic depressions. The neurotic or reactive depression is usually milder and is a reaction to a real loss, such as the death of a loved one or the loss of something considered valuable. But the individual overreacts—mourns excessively, may have difficulty in sleeping and eating, and is usually completely unaware that he is furious about the loss of the person or possession. In a psychotic depression, the loss and the possible source of anger may be more obscure. These people are usually much sicker, more withdrawn, and sometimes actively suicidal. One type of psychotic depression is known as manic-depressive psychosis. The cause of this is not known but is suspected to be either genetic or biochemical. Two other forms of psychotic depression, however, may be related to unacknowledged anger. One is the so-called postpartum psychosis, a depression that occurs after the birth of a child. Although the mother is expected to be happy at such a time, some women develop a severe depression. This may be caused by the feeling that she has lost the child she was carrying in her body—a particularly valuable possession, and it may also result from fear and anger at having to take the life-and-death responsibility for a helpless infant.

Perhaps a more understandable psychotic depression is so-called involutional melancholia. This occurs at the time of menopause. It is more common in women although it may occur in men as well. Here the relationship to repressed anger is more apparent. Now that the menstrual periods have stopped, the woman is no longer able to bear children, a primary function in a woman's life, and she may feel that she is useless and her whole life is over. Although these feelings are symptoms of depression, beneath them is a tremendous anger. She is forced to face the facts that part of her life really is over and that she is growing old and may no longer be attractive and desirable. Some women also feel that their sexual life is now finished. This is not true physiologically; some women find that they enjoy sex more. It has been fairly well established that there is no reason for a woman to lose enjoyment of sex after the menopause, and if she had previously been inhibited because she was constantly concerned about getting pregnant, she may now be able to relax and enjoy it fully.

Involutional depression occurs less frequently with men. It also comes on later in life—in the sixties and seventies—and is usually less severe. While loss of the ability to perform sexually is a major factor, men often have an outlet for their creative drives in their work, so that sexual impairment is less significant and therefore does not usually stir up so much anger. However, if his work is also removed, a man may go into a depression unless he has something active and meaningful with which to occupy himself. This is a serious consideration in relation to retirement. Studies have shown that old people placed in homes where they have little to do, do not live as long as those who remain active. Retiring, in itself, can affect health and survival.

It should also be noted that loss of male sexual ability, even in the sixties and seventies, is largely emotional. If men believe that they will lose their sexual drive they are more likely to do so. Physiologically, men can continue to have erections in their eighties and nineties.

It is important to recognize that depressions can occur in all of us. We are usually able to throw them off, particularly if we can resolve the issues which led to them—often sources of anger. If this is not done and the anger accumulates, a serious depression requiring hospitalization and drastic treatment may ensue.

suicide

Suicide, which is the ultimate expression of anger turned against the self, is a major hazard in the health of our society today. It is impossible to collect accurate statistics on the incidence of suicide. Estimates for the United States range from 10,000 to 30,000 per year. However, many suicides are never recorded as such, and the incidence may be at least two or three times as great. Not only are deaths reported as accidental when they were really intentional, but often the person himself is unaware that he is committing suicide. How frequently it has been said of someone who is exceedingly reckless, "He is trying to kill himself." One can only guess at the number of people who die in automobile accidents and drug overdoses because of their basic wish to kill themselves. Such a drive may exist in the drug addict as well as the alcoholic. The latter is often described as "drinking himself to death." The drive may be more subtle in the obese person who is "eating himself to death."

Suicide is not a problem affecting only adults. Nowadays younger and younger people are attempting to destroy themselves. Suicide has been reported in ten- and twelve-year-olds and even younger children. Among college students, suicide and automobile accidents are the two most frequent causes of death. Many studies on suicide are now being conducted, including some in primitive cultures such as the Eskimo, and undoubtedly much can be learned from these. However, the role of anger in self-destruction must be considered carefully.

As this chapter shows, anger of which we are unaware can be extremely harmful to us both physically and mentally and can even cause death, either through irreversible physical change or by suicide. When anger is turned outward, it becomes destructive of external things, including human lives, and the whole problem of violence in our society arises.

VI

anger and society

IN RECENT YEARS THERE HAS BEEN A GROWING concern about the increase in overt violence in our society, and many efforts have been made to understand this phenomenon. The factors involved include social and cultural problems as well as political and economic ones, all of which are beyond the scope of this book. However, one factor that must be considered basic is anger in the individual. Violence in a group does not occur unless the individuals in the group are angry. If we can prevent the anger of the individuals, we can prevent the violence.

The history of nations trying to live with one another is a continuous chronicle of anger and hostility. The violence of wars is obvious, but there could be no wars unless soldiers were willing to fight. War is probably the most important factor in determining the fate of nations. What is the role of man and his emotions in wars?

Wars are made by men, and something in man must respond to the violence and savagery they unleash. As has been mentioned, along with his sexual instinct man has an aggressive, destructive instinct. Just as he must control his sexual drives, he must channelize his hostile impulses. Most men adapt to the demands of civilized society that they not be openly destructive but redirect this energy to achieve social goals and also to provide satisfactions for themselves.

Now along comes a war. Civilized society now says not only that it is acceptable for men to kill but that it is their duty to their country. Man now finds himself in a situation where his aggressive instincts can have open and honorable expression. We have worked so hard at repressing these impulses that it is sometimes hard to believe they exist and that an outlet for them could prove enjoyable. Yet observe how children love to destroy things. Adults are often unable to comprehend this pleasure.

In a sense, sending a man to war is comparable to putting him in a room full of beautiful women and telling him he can do whatever he likes with them—that, in fact, this is his duty to his country. The wild fulfillment of the sexual drive is probably more easily recognized as pleasurable because society has not demanded as much repression of the sexual drive as of the aggressive one. Complete sexual expression is normal and accepted in marriage and is becoming widely accepted between two consenting partners. Full expression of aggression, as in killing another person, is not accepted in any society—except in war.

It can be argued that wars are waged, not out of anger but for power or economic reasons. But the leaders know that they must appeal to men's aggressive qualities to get them to fight. The most successful wars have been won by presenting a cause calling for the vindication of national honor. Such a cause is acceptable enough to break down the wall against releasing aggression and to turn civilized men into destructive machines. There were relatively few protests against the Second World War. Americans were furious at Hitler's aggression and his oppression of the Jews and of conquered countries and at the Japanese for attacking Pearl Harbor—very "righteous" causes.

In the wars in Southeast Asia it has not been possible to whip up as much anger in the American people, and as a result much more opposition has developed, with many men refusing to go. Fighting a war merely to prevent the spread of communism does not seem to be appealing enough to overcome the resistance against open expression of our destructive drives. But if Americans can be convinced that our country has been dishonored, the barriers may break. Many wars have been fought to avenge a wrong. The reputed cause of the Trojan War was the Greek desire for vengeance on Paris and Troy for the abduction of a queen. Numerous lives have been lost because a country or a flag was insulted.

History is full of brutalities committed by leaders against their own people or those they have conquered. The torture and violence that leaders of so-called civilized nations have inflicted on their people indicate the power of hostile impulses when these are given the opportunity to be expressed. The Egyptians enslaved and tormented the Hebrews. The Romans made slaves of the Christians and tortured them in all sorts of ways. Museums have collections of torture devices, which are beyond belief. It is interesting to see how many people visit these museums and are obviously intrigued by their contents. In modern times the destruction of six million Jews by the Hitler regime suggests that civilization has done very little to modify the destructive instincts of man. Many Africans have recently been slaughtered by their compatriots in the name of establishing the "proper" government. The history of the present Russian government is stained with the blood of thousands who were destroyed as enemies of the people. Such barbaric behavior in so-called civilized people reaffirms its instinctual basis.

In many religious movements anger has been a major

force, both in reasons for starting religions (various sects breaking away from the mother church, for example) and in the competition between groups, each feeling it has the only truth and the acceptance of this must be imposed, by force if necessary, on everyone else. In early religions, unexplainable natural events such as lightning and thunder were believed to be due to the anger of the gods, and primitive peoples were constantly appeasing this wrath by sacrifices, including human ones. Although the Judaic God was a great advance over the primitive divinities, he was still thought of as an angry, revengeful deity. Moses had to dissuade the Lord from destroying the Israelites when they set up images. The Lord said, "Let me alone, that my wrath may wax hot against them, and that I may consume them." One of the major changes in the Christian ethic was from the "eye for an eye, tooth for a tooth" philosophy of the earlier religion to the concept of "turning the other cheek." Yet even the Prince of Peace, when He was in great physical torment on the cross, cried out, "My God, my God, why hast thou forsaken me?", a statement of protest which basically is an angry one.

The various religious crusades are examples of the extensive use of hostility in the name of religion. Inquisitions, witch-hunting, and religious persecutions have long been socially accepted outlets for mass brutality. This is not to say that religion is merely hostile and destructive; on the contrary, among the most effective codes of ethical behavior are those developed by organized religions. But as groups evolve, many factors come into play, and anger is one of the powerful ones.

What goes on among the people in our society today? People are frequently cruel to one another, as they always have been. They rob each other, attack each other, and murder each other. All this has been going on as long as people have been living together. Studies vary as to whether violence has actually increased or whether we are simply more aware of it. With radio and television, more information is readily available to more people. Some of the military have stated that the war in Southeast Asia is no more violent than any other, but with television on the front lines, people are now actually seeing what has always gone on. Data on murders, rapes, and violent crimes is now more accurate than in the past but there is some doubt that the actual incidence of these crimes has increased. There may be an increase in actual numbers, but since the population has also increased, the percentage may be the same.

Is there anything that understanding of anger and its origins can contribute toward solving today's problems? We know that healthy outlets for aggression can be developed and should be encouraged. These range from constructive uses to recreational ones. The aggressive drives and accumulated angers of mankind can neither be denied nor destroyed; they are bound to come out in some form. Directing them toward useful activities is the best way of handling them.

A second important lesson is that certain specific things generate anger in everyone and if we are aware of these we may be able to avoid them, thus decreasing the amount of anger we must cope with. An outstanding generator of anger is frustration. One way to decrease violence in our society is to remove the source of frustration inherent in social and economic inequalities. Prejudice, poverty, and unequal opportunities are injustices that must be corrected. However, in our efforts to do so, we have introduced a new factor which simply adds to the frustration. Its avoidance, in my opinion, could help us diminish the anger of the already exceedingly frustrated minority groups.

For hundreds of years the black people in America were enslaved and oppressed. Naturally they resented and hated their condition, but any open expression of violence was brutally suppressed. They learned to deal with their hostilities in less violent ways, by withdrawing, becoming apathetic, and regressing in their behavior. When anger overwhelmed them, they tended to take it out on one another. Only occasionally did it break out against society.

After the slaves were freed, to be black continued to be considered to be inferior, and tragically this attitude has persisted, even among many blacks. Not too long ago, a group of black children was given a choice between black dolls and white ones. They prefered the white ones.

As our society became more enlightened, it was increasingly recognized that this attitude was terribly wrong, and civil rights groups developed to work for equal rights for blacks. In their zeal to redress the wrongs, they indicated to the blacks that they had a right to instant equality. Unfortunately, our society was not capable of delivering this, because of the sheer mechanics of the situation. Prejudice against blacks was still widespread; educational systems were not geared to give equal training; health care was unequally distributed; jobs did not exist; housing conditions for many blacks were deplorable. When the demands for immediate correction of all inequalities were frustrated, tremendous anger was generated, superimposed on that already existing. Violence began to erupt, which stimulated fear and anger among the whites and increased their prejudice against the blacks. Greater frustration, anger, and violence on the part of blacks followed. Building up the expectation of immediate solutions only exacerbated the problems. When the blacks were told that it would take time to work these things out, they resented this tremendously and became more violent as a reaction. No one can blame them for this, but the reality is that, even if all prejudice could be instantly removed, which of course it cannot, the blacks cannot be instantly educated and trained for better paying jobs, houses cannot be instantly built or redistributed, wealth cannot instantly be more equitably distributed, and self-value cannot be instantly restored. The more stress on immediate equalization, the worse the frustration and anger. This frustration is being increased by groups whose intention is only to do good. Now that there is evidence that society generally recognizes the gross inequities and is working toward their correction with the help of the civil rights groups, perhaps the violence need only be a transitional phase. Obviously, a great deal of cooperation on the part of all the people is required. Violence does not usually lead to cooperation. Groups seeking equal rights for blacks and other minorities must work with society to accomplish this goal instead of making demands impossible to satisfy.

The goal must be to remove as many as possible of the frustrations imposed by our society and to do so as quickly as possible. Malnutrition and poverty must be abolished; housing must be made decent; people must have equal opportunities for education and jobs. These are social and economic problems which must be solved by social and economic means. One way of hastening the process may be to avoid adding to the real frustrations by creating unrealistic hopes.

Everyone has a right to be angry about the inequities in

our society. Prejudice and unfairness are causes for real anger, and we must all use the energy of this real anger toward correcting these faults. However, promises that cannot be fulfilled create additional anger which is not realistic. The excessive quantity of unrealistic anger not only generates violence but prevents many from using this energy constructively.

Enormous as are the frustrations of inadequate food, poor housing, and poverty, perhaps the greatest source of anger in oppressed minorities is lack of dignity and self-respect. True equality must include not only acceptance by others but an inner recognition of one's own equality by the individual. Just as every boy must be convinced of his manliness and every girl of her lovability, every minority child must be convinced of his equal value. If this problem is not solved, the anger generated either turns outward, where it is released in violence, or inward where it is so painful that some escape is necessary. This need may be an important factor in the increased use of drugs and alcohol.

One of the important ingredients in prejudice is that a person who feels inferior can make himself feel superior by declaring someone else inferior. A man six feet tall may say that a man five feet tall is shorter than he. That is not prejudice; it is fact. But if the six-foot-tall man feels inferior or threatened with a loss of power or material things, he may say being short is a sign of weakness, sexual inferiority, and poor intellect. This is prejudice. Since we all start life with feelings of inferiority, prejudice is common and deeply rooted. If the tall man insists on his claims, the short man will become angry. If the short man fights the prejudices or proves them wrong, the tall man gets angry. The tall man not only has

anger from the frustration but now has an outlet for his accumulated anger from many sources, and the short man is
blamed for everything the tall man resents. Prejudice thus
provides an outlet for a great deal of hostility.

The violence which I have been discussing is primarily
group action and does not explain most of the individual
destructive acts reported in the press. These acts are usually
committed by emotionally sick people in response to their
sickness. Many are psychotic, some schizophrenic. They may
believe that they are being persecuted and must get rid of
their tormentors (paranoia), or that voices tell them to perpe-
trate the crimes (auditory hallucinations), or that they are an
all-powerful people destined to save the world (delusions of
grandeur).

Hostilities exist not only between nations and religious
groups but also between groups within groups. Competition
and efforts to seize power can generate tremendous anger
between Republicans and Democrats, capital and labor,
North and South, cities and rural areas, states and federal
government. While the hostility is usually confined to verbal
expression, violence not infrequently breaks out. The history
of the labor movement in this country is full of violent action.
The hostility between North and South ended in civil war.

Among smaller units, feuds between families were well
known when families were more closely knit groups than they
are today. The Montagus and Capulets in *Romeo and Juliet* are
an example; so are the blood feuds in the Southern moun-
tains.

Within the family constellation itself, hostilities have ex-
isted since families developed. When Adam and Eve had two
sons, one slew the other. Hamlet's father was killed by his

brother and Hamlet himself kills his stepfather-uncle as well as the father of his sweetheart. In most of the great tragedies of literature the violent acts occur within the family. Lizzie Borden was acquitted, but according to a ballad of the time, she "took an axe and gave her mother forty whacks; when she saw what she had done, she gave her father forty-one." Husbands and wives have destroyed each other since the beginning of time. Children have turned against parents, and parents against children. Studies of murders show that the victim is usually known to and often related to the murderer, being a husband, a wife, a parent, or a sweetheart.

The crucial question is, what can be done about all this anger?

VII

what to do about anger

WHEN THE QUESTION OF ANGER ARISES IN treatment, patients often say, "Okay, I know I'm angry. What do I do about it? Do I punch my wife in the nose? Is that what you're advising?" They sometimes show great hostility toward me because they believe I am suggesting that their anger should be expressed directly and openly toward the person who has aroused it. They often feel, and correctly, that the open expression of anger will not solve the problem.

There are no simple solutions to the problems of anger and no pat formulas for dealing with the complex issues involved. However, there are four steps which, if they can be followed through, may lead to a reasonable resolution of the anger.

recognize that you are angry

The first step in dealing with anger is to recognize that you are angry and admit it to yourself. Anger of which we are aware is much less harmful than unrecognized or unadmitted anger. It is essential that we uncover the feelings first. This is not easy. People will continue to speak of being disappointed, frustrated, let down, unaware that these expressions may indicate repressed anger. Emotions are repressed because they are unacceptable. Anger may be denied because we feel too guilty about it or are afraid of it. The conflict between the anger and the guilt may be completely unconscious. If we try to bring out these feelings, they may be held in tighter than ever, because they were unacceptable in the first place, and trying to reveal them openly will only increase the resistance to their exposure.

Thus in seeking to recognize anger we must be aware that often we cannot attack the problem directly. However, there are many clues to hidden anger. If you are tense and don't know why, or have any of the disguised manifestations of anger described earlier, you should explore the possibility that you are angry and not aware of it. If you feel depressed, ask yourself what you might be angry about. Until you can recognize the anger, you cannot decide what to do about it. Meanwhile the anger will continue to hurt you. When I say to a patient, "It sounds to me as if you are angry about something," and he replies, angrily, "Okay, I'm angry. What do I do about it?" the answer is that he can do nothing about it because he has not yet truly recognized that he is angry. Until he recognizes that the problem is anger that he is not accepting, the whole process stops. Sometimes the anger is so threatening and unacceptable to an individual that he cannot recognize it by any of the means suggested in this chapter, and he may need professional help. However, if you are feeling sad, unhappy, fed up, annoyed, hurt, harassed, and talking about being frustrated, disappointed, ready to explode, or using any of the other expressions that hint at hidden anger, perhaps you should ask yourself, "Am I angry about something? What is it? Am I afraid to face the situation? Am I afraid to face the anger? Is the situation one that I really shouldn't be angry about but am anyway?

Remember that anger frequently is not reasonable, but that does not mean that it does not exist. Emotions are not governed by reason. People usually do not fall in love reasonably. Patients will say to me, "How can I be angry when I have no right to be?" In psychiatric treatment it is a common experience for the patient to develop angry feelings toward the doctor. However, if you ask a patient to talk about this, he will say, "I'm not angry at you, because you have given me no cause to be angry." This is being reasonable. But the patient may nevertheless be feeling anger because the doctor in some way represents a father toward whom the patient had enormous hostility, and this is now transferred onto the doctor. The patient cannot face or deal with his anger because he cannot find a "real" reason for it. This does not negate the anger, however. It is a serious error to insist that you cannot be angry because this does not seem reasonable. What is important and entirely reasonable is to look within yourself for anger that you have not been recognizing. In attempting to recognize anger it is necessary to be aware that feelings of guilt or of unreasonableness must not deter you from looking for the clues. If the guilt or the sense that the anger is unjustified makes you pass judgment on these feelings you will not get beyond this first step. Anger is an emotional phenomenon and can be dealt with only when you are aware of it as an emotion. To be aware of it purely intellectually is not more than one third of the way to truly recognizing it. One cannot simply say, "I must be angry since I am feeling frustrated or disappointed." One must go on to say, "I am frustrated, and

that—damn it—*does* make me angry!" In the second instance
you are really beginning to feel the anger, which is what is
meant by recognizing it. If you have any of the manifestations
of hidden anger you must suspect that anger may be playing
a role in producing them. Such indirect expressions as acci-
dent-proneness or depression can escape through the barrier
of the unconscious, but they do not directly give away the
anger. However, they can be utilized to lead to the real problem which may be the hidden anger. Once you can feel the
anger and can accept the fact that you are angry, you are now
ready to move on to the second step.

identify the source
of the anger

Once you have recognized that you are angry, you have taken
the most difficult step. Then the problem is to try to understand where the anger is coming from. This may be very
obvious, or it may be very subtle. If someone deliberately
steps on my foot, I don't have to look far to find the source
of my anger. If the baby drops my favorite statue and breaks
it, the anger may seem less reasonable ("he's only a baby"),
but the cause is still fairly clear. If a man flirts with my wife,
I may be angry with him, or with her, or both.

However, the sources may be difficult to ferret out if the
real instigator of the anger is someone who is powerful or who
can harm us in some way and with whom, therefore, it is not
prudent to be angry. We tend to handle such a situation by
looking for another possible source on which to blame the

anger. This is known as displacement, and we usually do it unconsciously. You may be angry at your boss for the way he treats you at work but say that you are angry with your wife because she is neglecting you at home. This is, of course, a simple example. You may feel that to be angry at your boss threatens your job, so you snarl at your wife because she has spoiled the meal, but when the anger is out of proportion to the cause, you must suspect that it is an outlet for anger generated by someone or something else.

Another common reason for displacing anger is to avoid humiliating or belittling yourself. If you take a wrong turn in the road, you may blame your wife for distracting you or misguiding you, though the mistake was really due to your own carelessness. An even more obvious example is kicking the door you bump into. It certainly was not the door's fault. A woman may get furious with her husband if he comments that another woman is attractive, when her anger really comes from feeling that she is not as attractive as the other woman or is threatened by her.

Guilt can also confuse the real source of anger. A man may be furious with his mother, but because one must not get angry with one's mother, he may find himself exploding at other older women, sometimes wondering himself why he is *so* angry with them.

A variation of this is what I call "the road to anger is paved with good intentions" syndrome. A stockbroker goes out of his way to give you a hot tip on the market. You buy the stock and lose money. How can you be angry with the broker, who meant only to make money for you? Yet you lost money, and you are furious. You are in a bind, however, because his intentions were the best. This is, perhaps, one of the most difficult sources of anger for people to deal with. Many patients have said to me, "So my mother kept me a little boy and never let me grow up. She did everything for me. She never let me make any decisions or take responsibility. No girl was ever good enough for me. But she thought she was doing the right thing. How can I be angry with her?" But the fury at having been emotionally crippled by these good intentions is often there.

The second step, then, is to recognize the true source of your anger. It may be obvious, or appear to be obvious, but really be displaced from some other source. In order to be able to deal with it, the real cause must be ascertained. An important clue is more anger toward a person or situation than is realistically warranted. One should then suspect that the real anger is directed at another person, but because of fear or guilt must be denied and is let out on someone else.

understand why you are angry

Now that you recognize your anger and know where it is coming from, the next step is to try to understand *why* you are angry. If someone steps on your foot you are angry because you have physical pain. If you are a woman and a strange man takes liberties with you at a party, pinching you or fondling you, you are angry because he is taking advantage of you. However, even in apparently simple situations the reason may be harder to find. Someone throws a ball and it hits you on the head, inflicting severe pain. The man who threw the ball apologizes, and you accept his apology, realizing he did not mean to hurt you. Nevertheless, you are angry, because, when someone inflicts pain, even if he did not intend to do so and is upset about it, anger results, and should be recognized. In the "road to anger is paved with good intentions" syndrome, we are angry because we have been hurt, physically, financially, emotionally, or however. The woman who is angry at the man who took liberties with her may really be angry because she wanted him to do so and he is exposing a repressed wish, or because she wonders if she unconsciously led him on and that makes her feel guilty.

A more difficult case is that of Sue, who was afraid to walk outside alone. Sue was a twenty-two-year-old woman who had agoraphobia (fear of being in open places or crowds). She hated her mother but was completely unaware of this feeling. Sue's mother had not wanted children and had had Sue only to please her husband. When he died two years after the child was born, the mother was left with the burden of supporting and raising her. She had resented this very much but felt guilty at having such unmotherly feelings, so the feelings were pushed down into her unconscious, and she became overly solicitous toward Sue. Overreaction is a common way of denying the opposite true feeling. It is used particularly to deny anger. The saccharine sweet person is not really sweet at all but a bitter, angry individual, and because we sense this we find such people unpleasant and uncomfortable to be with. Sue sensed her mother's rejection of her and resentment of her as a burden and was stifled by her mother's overprotection. This generated anger, which she could not express because mother was always so solicitous, which accumulated until she developed neurotic symptoms, including not being able to go anywhere without her mother.

On the surface it would appear that Sue needed her mother constantly by her side because she loved her and was afraid to be away from her. But the effect on the mother was not exactly a loving one. She had to devote her whole life to her daughter, at great sacrifice and undoubtedly with much hidden resentment. The daughter, on the other hand, had an almost perfect solution to her problem. She was angry with her mother for not really loving her, but she could not openly express this and was, in fact, an unduly well-behaved child. By requiring that her mother be with her at all times, she could still appear to be a good little girl who loved her mother very much, but she was making life extremely unpleasant for mother, thus giving an outlet to her own deep anger. When Sue finally understood why she was angry, she was able to figure out ways to handle it.

This is an example of the ingenious way in which hidden anger can be used by the unconscious. On the surface all is loving, but underneath the anger is constantly boiling and eventually comes through. To the world, Sue was such a devoted daughter that she could not bear to be without her mother. In reality, the mother had no life of her own and was completely miserable, not only because she was unable to move without her daughter but also because all her efforts had resulted in a sick, disabled child.

Perhaps the most important question about why we are angry is whether the reason is realistic. If you are angry at the boss because he is paying you $1.00 an hour when the minimum is $1.50, this is a realistic reason. If you are angry because he is not giving you special consideration, this is not realistic. We often experience anger because we have taken as personal something that may not be personal at all. A driver may cut in front of you in a traffic line. You get furious at him, but why? It is important to recognize that he is not doing it to you personally; he would probably do it to anyone. You have a right to be angry at his careless driving, but if you take the incident personally it can release a great deal of resentment. You should say, "How can he do that stupid thing?"—which is realistic and appropriate—not "How can he do that stupid thing to me?"—which is unrealistic and infuriating. The essence of the third step is to attempt to determine why you are angry and to decide whether the reason is realistic or not. Anger for unrealistic reasons—usually hidden feelings, wishes, or expectations—is difficult to face and deal with.

deal with the anger realistically

The fourth step is probably the easiest because it follows naturally from the other three. If we have recognized that we are angry, know the source of the anger, and have found that the cause is a realistic one, then we must deal with the anger realistically. If someone pushes ahead of you in a line, it is reasonable to ask him to go back to the end of the line; it is not realistic just to swallow your anger.

Obviously, however, a direct expression of the anger is not always the best solution. When you know who has made you angry and why and that the anger has a reasonable cause, a confrontation with the person provoking the anger may resolve the problem. If you are dissatisfied with the pay that your boss is giving you and it is reasonable to expect higher pay, the solution is not to go home and complain to your wife but to try to arrive at an understanding with your boss. If this is unsatisfactory or impracticable and you must put up with the situation, it may be necessary to find other outlets for the energy. However, you must not deny to yourself that you are furious. Once the anger is out in the open as far as you yourself are concerned, it is much less likely to cause problems for you. If other outlets for the energy are not effective, it may be necessary to change the situation that is creating the anger, even if this entails giving up some advantages.

Anger is more difficult to deal with when the cause of it is not realistic. Here the basic problem is within yourself and may require a good deal of effort and patience to solve. If you are angry at your wife because she is not treating you as your mother always did, you need to recognize that your wife is not your mother and really should not act as if she were. If you insist that she do so and get angry if she does not, you have to figure out why you need to have your wife be a mother to you. It is easy to suggest recognizing that your wife is not your mother, but if the need is deep-seated, the attitude may be difficult to eradicate. Sometimes professional help is required.

Usually the problem is not so simple. The wife probably also has problems and may be contributing to the situation. It may be very difficult for a man to decide whether his anger at his wife is because she is not mothering him or has realistic causes. The situation can be further complicated by the mechanism called rationalization, which we all use. If the man is really angry at his wife because she is not mothering him but in addition she is a sloppy housekeeper, he points out only the second fact as the cause of his anger. However, the tipoff is that the anger is often greater than the situation calls for.

The best way to resolve many such situations is by increased communication. It is important for a man and his wife to discuss their feelings in an effort to arrive at a reasonable solution. If husband or wife has been accumulating anger without recognizing it, this anger can interfere with communication and make it extremely difficult to come to grips with the real problem. It is simple enough to say that if anger has a realistic cause it should be dealt with realistically; if it has an unreasonable or unrealistic source, the real cause must be found before the anger can be dealt with. Determining the actual cause can be extremely complex but an example from everyday life may be helpful.

A housewife with three children notices that she is feeling exhausted, bored with housework, irritable with the children, and restless. She is more tired in the morning than when she went to bed. She is having trouble sleeping and is overeating. If she were asked how she feels, she would say that she has a great deal of work to do and that it is getting her down. Physical check-ups have shown that her health is normal. The first step is to understand that her feelings are coming from anger. She is not tired from physical overwork alone. She is not having trouble sleeping merely because she is worried about the children. She is not overeating because there is nothing else to do. Her difficulties are caused by hidden anger. Now she must try to understand what she is angry about, which is not difficult to determine, but it may be extremely difficult to accept. Housework is dull and unrewarding. She picks up after the children and an hour later has to do it again.

Her work never reaches a point where she can say even to herself, "See what I have accomplished!" Her husband is absorbed in his job, which either may be satisfying to him or create problems which he complains about to his wife. He is unaware of the amount of work she does, and if she complains, he withdraws. This, of course, makes her still more angry. He in turn may yell at her that she doesn't realize how hard he works. She complains more, he withdraws more, and they reinforce each other's anger. However, if she can recognize her frustration and discouragement, she has found the source of her anger.

Now she must decide how realistic the anger is. If there are ways of reducing the burdens of housework and children and she is not using them, perhaps her anger comes from something else. Perhaps she feels that her husband has been growing less attentive and that this is because she is becoming less attractive, being overwhelmed by all the work and not having an opportunity to take care of herself. Perhaps she wanted to have a career in the outside world and now feels that she is accomplishing nothing, or at least nothing that anyone gives her credit for. Until she has truly figured out why she is angry and whether the cause is realistic or not, she cannot deal with the anger.

When the fact of anger, the source, and the reason, have all been brought into the open, the question is what can be done about it? She can leave home, she can beat the children, she can scream at her husband that he does not appreciate or love her. This is direct action and usually not effective. She can continue to eat excessively. She can escape through television. (The appeal of soap operas is that they make us think our own troubles are not really so bad.) She can go to the movies. She can look for an outside romance. None of these is a satisfactory solution.

A better approach would be to say to herself, "I am furious about my life because I'm getting no satisfaction from it. It doesn't help to say that I can't blame my children, because they are only children, or my poor husband, because he must make a living. I am still frustrated and angry. How can I get some constructive satisfaction out of life?" If she can talk with her husband and get him to recognize what her feelings are, this is an excellent beginning. But she must not talk with her husband in an angry way, as though the problem is his fault. The goal is to develop an attitude of "looking for something together." Then the wife can try to make some realistic decisions. Perhaps she should take a part-time job and pay a baby sitter, even if financially this means only breaking even. The satisfaction of doing something that she feels is visibly productive can give her a sense of accomplishment that will be highly gratifying.

Many mothers of young children fear that being away from their children will hurt them emotionally. Certainly a very young child needs its mother, but a child of three or four can tolerate separation from her for a few hours a day. In fact, the mother who spends some time away from her children may be doing them a favor. Because she has been getting satisfaction in another situation, the hours spent with the children, though fewer, will be happier. If her husband can recognize that being more considerate of his wife will improve his home life, he will realize the value of investing the time and effort this may require. If he is completely self-centered and cannot see the problem or simply continues to get angry with her, other steps may be necessary to change his attitude.

Once there is communication and understanding, the wife must make a personal search to discover her particular interests and what can be done to express them within the framework of her life.

A number of these factors are illustrated by Jack's case. Jack was a thirty-one-year-old hardware executive who had developed viral symptoms. He had been given a thorough medical check-up, in which no serious organic causes were found. After three months he felt completely exhausted and finally came to see me because he had thoughts of killing himself. When he came into the office, he did not appear particularly depressed, but he was tense and could not sit still in the chair. He began by saying that he couldn't understand how he could possibly have thought of jumping out of a window when he really had nothing to be depressed about. He said, "I have a good business, with a fine future. My wife is devoted to me; we have one child and are expecting a second, which we have wanted very much." Jack was a born salesman, appeared to like everyone, and indicated that he did not have an enemy in the world. "If my friends knew that I'd had any thoughts about suicide, they really would think that I had flipped." At first, Jack expressed only praise for his boss Oscar and gratitude for the opportunity to make such fine progress in a growing, successful business. It took Jack some time to perceive that his persistent somatic symptoms and unexpected thoughts of suicide indicated how furious and frustrated he really felt. One of the important things that he had to overcome was the apparent unreasonableness of this rage, since his gratitude toward Oscar was genuine. But along with these positive feelings he had been accumulating more and more anger from the frustration of feeling that

Oscar was holding him back. There were several reasons for this anger. The first and obvious one was Jack's frustration at being treated like a little boy. The second was that this tapped a large reservoir of anger that he had accumulated toward his father, who had also frequently belittled him and made him feel small and helpless. As a result, Jack had unconsciously resolved to surpass his father. He was therefore very competitive and eager to be the top man in the business. Since this was not what Oscar wanted, Jack was again frustrated. Thus he had at least three reasons for being so angry at his boss. The first was realistic: his boss was treating him as a young, somewhat incompetent junior partner. The other two were unrealistic, since they were related to his anger toward his father and the frustration at not being able to compete successfully with the older man. Eventually he was able to deal with the realistic problem by a confrontation with his boss, who had become more aware of Jack's value when he was out sick and was eager to do what he could to help. By recognizing that his boss was not his father and that he really did not have to surpass him in order to prove his own worth, Jack was able to deal more effectively with his life situation. While other factors in Jack's life contributed to his problem, he succeeded in recognizing the anger, in ascertaining its sources and the reasons it was generated, and finally in deciding what to do about it.

Dealing with other people's anger is an aspect of the anger problem which may be very difficult. If your wife is angry and this causes you to respond with anger of your own, further anger will be aroused in her, and a cycle may be set up which simply keeps the anger going. One of you must break the cycle by stopping the angry reaction. The problem here is that each partner feels that the other should be the one to back off. However, the real question is whether you want to resolve the problem or to get the momentary satisfaction of hurting each other by expressing anger directly. Again reasonable communication is essential, and unless you can both calm down and discuss the issues, the problem cannot be resolved. Recognizing that you react in anger toward the anger expressed by the other person can put you in a position to deal with your anger, not necessarily by expressing it openly, but by recognizing its existence and consciously controlling it. Open anger can interfere with the resolution of a problem; on the other hand, hidden anger expressed indirectly is equally provocative. If a husband expresses anger toward his wife and she responds in a condescending, patronizing, or sarcastic way, which she considers her way of being calm, this may stir up more anger in him. Any of these attitudes is a method of expressing anger, which the other person recognizes.

It is not possible to generalize about dealing with the type of violent anger shown by a person who threatens you with a gun or knife. The usual advice is to keep calm and give the individual what he wants rather than angering him further, but this is sometimes very difficult to do. Books of instructions are now being provided for officers of the law on how to handle violent people. Generally, they are urged to stay calm and attempt to be reassuring while at the same time carrying out their duties. Anger and threats usually provoke further hostility in the enraged person.

The four steps in dealing with anger are easy enough to describe but less easy to carry out. It would be nice if one could say, "Now that I have gone through the various steps, all my problems will be solved." Unfortunately, life is much more complex than this. Gus came to see me because he was severely depressed, and he actually required a short period of hospitalization. It became clear that Gus's problem was his tremendous fury at his wife. She made little effort to communicate with him or to show the love and attention that he had hoped for in marriage. She was sexually cold and did only the bare essentials in caring for the house. Having worked out the steps of knowing he was angry and understanding why, he still had to go home to a wife who was not communicative, demonstrative, or affectionate. For many reasons, however, he wanted to preserve the marriage, and he was apparently back in his old dilemma and on the surface no better off than he had been before treatment. However, there was one big difference which was to his advantage. Instead of feeling that this was the way marriages were, that his wife was behaving as a wife should, and that he should feel guilty about objecting to her behavior, he was now able to recognize his anger and to decide what he could do about the situation. Being aware of his anger did not keep him from wishing that his wife would change, but he was able to look for other solutions. He became interested in sailing, motorboating, and golf, and took special courses to improve his skills. He also joined a book club. He demanded less from his relationship with his wife, and consequently was less frustrated. When he was with his wife the relationship was more agreeable because he was not so angry with her. One of the problems Gus had to work through was his resentment because he had to make all the changes. He would often ask, "Why can't she change some; why does it always have to be me?" The practical answer was that he had to make the changes because he was the one who had been made sick by the existing situation. His wife apparently was functioning reasonably well. The issue was not fairness but practicality. If he had refused to make all the changes because this appeared to place all the blame on him, he would have continued to be frustrated and depressed. Some people unfortunately sacrifice their health and happiness on the altar of justice. Justice is an elusive ideal. If a situation bothers you, the best thing to do is to make the changes necessary for your own comfort. Insisting that blame be placed where it belongs and that the person at fault must be the one to change may only lead to further unhappiness. While Gus still felt that his wife was at fault, he recognized his anger, including the anger at having to make the changes, and then found realistic ways of coping. He continued to have mild episodes of depression, but he managed to live with them.

Understanding your own anger will not enable you to handle all the angers of the world, but at least you will know how to keep your own from working against you. If this book has helped you to identify the destructive forces within you, you as an individual will be better equipped not only to deal constructively with your own anger but to understand the angers so prevalent in society today. No one person can solve them all and you may not be able to handle them as well as you would like, but you will be able to cope with them more effectively because you have one less problem to deal with: your own hidden anger.

suggestions for further reading

index

SUGGESTIONS FOR
FURTHER READING

Aichhorn, August: *Wayward Youth*. New York: The Viking Press, 1935.

Alexander, Franz. *Psychosomatic Medicine*. New York: W.W. Norton, 1950.

Alexander, Franz, and Healy, William. *Roots of Crime: Psychoanalytic Studies*. Montclair, N.J.: Patterson Smith, 1969.

Brenner, Charles. *An Elementary Textbook of Psychoanalysis*. New York: International Universities Press, 1955.

Dunbar, Flanders. *Psychosomatic Diagnosis*. New York: Paul B. Hoeber, Inc., 1943.

Erikson, Erik. *Gandhi's Truth: On the Origins of Militant Nonviolence*. New York: W.W. Norton, 1969.

Freud, Anna, and Burlingham, Dorothy. *War and Children*. New York: International Universities Press, 1943.

Freud, Sigmund. *Beyond the Pleasure Principle*. Complete Psychological Works of Sigmund Freud, vol. 18. London: Hogarth Press, 1955.

———. *Jokes and Their Relation to the Unconscious*. Complete Psychological Works, vol. 8. London: Hogarth Press, 1960.

———. *New Introductory Lectures on Psychoanalysis*. Complete

Psychological Works, vol. 22. London: Hogarth Press, 1964. See chapter 32.

Hartman, H.; Kris, E.; and Loewenstein, R. "Notes on the Theory of Aggression," *Psychoanalytic Study of the Child*, vol. 3/4, 1949.

Lorenz, Konrad. *On Aggression*, New York: Harcourt, Brace & World, 1966.

Mark, V.H., and Ervin, F. *Violence and the Brain*, New York: Harper & Row, 1970.

Marmor, Judd. "War, Violence and Human Nature," *Bulletin of Atomic Scientists*, vol. 20, no. 3, 1964.

Menninger, Karl. *Love Against Hate*. New York: Harcourt, Brace & World, 1934.

————. *Man Against Himself*, New York: Harcourt, Brace & World, 1956.

Saul, Leon. *The Hostile Mind*. New York: Random House, 1956.

Selye, Hans. *The Stress of Life*. New York: McGraw-Hill, 1956.

Weiss, Edward, and English, O. Spurgeon. *Psychosomatic Medicine*. Philadelphia: W.B. Saunders Company, 1949.

Wolff, Harold. *Stress and Disease*. Springfield, Ill.: Charles C Thomas, 1968.

INDEX

INDEX

ABOUT THE AUTHOR

Leo Madow was born in Cleveland, Ohio. He received his B.A. from Western Reserve University, his M.A. (Psychology) from Ohio State University, and his M.D. from the Western Reserve University School of Medicine.

Dr. Madow is Professor and Chairman, Department of Psychiatry and Neurology, Medical College of Pennsylvania, Philadephia, and Consultant on the Staff of the Institute of the Pennsylvania Hospital for Mental and Nervous Diseases, Philadelphia. He is a past president of both the Philadelphia Psychoanalytic Society and the Philadelphia Psychiatric Society, Chairman of the Task Force on Mental Retardation of the American Psychiatric Association, and a former chairman of the Committee on Mental Retardation of the Group for the Advancement of Psychiatry. He is a Fellow of both the American Psychiatric Association and the American College of Physicians, a member of the American Neurological Association and the American Psycholanalytic Association as well as many other professional associations, and author of numerous scientific papers on neurology and psychiatry.

DATE DUE

MAR 2 5 2002			
MAY 0 5			
			Printed in USA